Listen all of you!

The priest of Hathor will beat twice any of you who

enters this tomb or does harm to it.

The gods will confront him because I am honored by his Lord.

The gods will not allow anything to happen to me.

Anyone who does anything bad to my tomb,

then the crocodile, hippopotamus, and lion will eat him.

— Curse inscription from the tomb of Petety

CURSE OF THE

My Adventures with Mummies
by ZAHI HAWASS

PHARAOHS

NATIONAL GEOGRAPHIC
WASHINGTON, D.C.

ACKNOWLEDGMENTS

THIS BOOK HAS BEEN PREPARED with the help of many friends and colleagues. I would like to thank Nina Hoffman, head of the book division at National Geographic, for her strong support and for making sure that the book looks wonderful. Thanks also to Susan Blair. My appreciation goes also to my dear friend Terry Garcia, Senior Vice President of the National Geographic Society. My thanks to my assistant, Mohamed Ismail, who collected slides and photos from my library, and to Brook Meyer and Sahar Mabrouk, both of whom help me in many ways. Finally, I would like to give my sincere thanks and admiration to my classmate, colleague, and friend, Janice Kamrin, who edited this book and helped me put down my stories so that readers can imagine they are hearing my voice.

Copyright © 2004 Zahi Hawass

Published by the National Geographic Society
John M. Fahey, Jr., *President and Chief Executive Officer*
Gilbert M. Grosvenor, *Chairman of the Board*
Nina D. Hoffman, *Executive Vice President,*
        President of Books and Education Publishing Group
Ericka Markman, *Senior Vice President,*
        President, Children's Books and Education
        Publishing Group

Staff for this book:
Nancy Laties Feresten, *Vice President,*
        Editor-in-Chief, Children's Books
Bea Jackson, *Art Director, Children's Books*
Marfé Ferguson Delano, *Project Editor*
Bea Jackson and Dan Sherman, *Designers*
Susan Blair, *Illustrations Editor*
Janet Dustin, *Illustrations Coordinator*
Carl Mehler, *Director of Maps*
Gregory Ugiansky, *Map Production*
Stuart Armstrong, *Map Illustration*
Connie D. Binder, *Indexer*
R. Gary Colbert, *Production Director*
Lewis R. Bassford, *Production Manager*
Vincent P. Ryan, *Manufacturing Manager*

Front cover: Spotlights lend an eerie glow to the head of a statue of Ramses II. The figure is one of four giant statues at his temple at Abu Simbel. A larger view of the temple appears on pages 96—97.
Back cover: Zahi Hawass stands in front of the Great Pyramid.
Front and back endsheets: These hieroglyphs were carved and painted on a coffin lid from the fourth century B.C.
Half-title page: This curse inscription was carved on the entrance to the tomb of Petety at Giza.
Title page: This gold death mask covered the head and shoulders of King Tutankhamun's mummy.
Title page (inset): Zahi Hawass takes a break in the tomb of Zed-khonsu-iuf-ankh.
Table of contents (left): Wrapped in linen and plaster, this mummy of a man called Waty lies in a tomb in Saqqara.
Table of contents (right): These figures decorate the ceiling of Ramses VI's tomb in the Valley of the Kings.

Library of Congress Cataloging-in-Publication Data
Hawass, Zahi A.
  Curse of the pharaohs : my adventures with mummies / by Zahi Hawass.--1st ed.
     p. cm.
Summary: Zahi A. Hawass, currently in charge of the Supreme Council of Antiquities in Egypt, tells true stories of archaeology and Egypt's treasures.
  1. Egypt--Antiquities--Juvenile literature. 2. Blessing and cursing--Egypt--Juvenile literature. 3. Hawass, Zahi A.--Juvenile literature. [1. Archaeology--Egypt. 2. Egypt--Antiquities. 3. Blessing and cursing. 4. Hawass, Zahi A.] I. Title.
  DT60.H385 2004
  932--dc22

                        2003018813

ISBN 0-7922-6665-X (trade edition)
ISBN 0-7922-6963-2 (library binding)

Illustrations Credits
Photographs by Kenneth Garrett, except as noted below:
ii-iii: Victor R. Boswell, Jr.; 5. Zahi Hawass Library; 8. Victor R. Boswell, Jr.; 14: Zahi Hawass Library; 15. Zahi Hawass Library; 18-19: Richard T. Nowitz; 24: Metropolitan Museum of Art; 27: Photography by Egyptian Expedition, MMA; 31: Archivo White Star; 32: Wide World; 33: Araldo de Luca/ Archivo White Star; 36: Hulton Archive/Getty Images; 37: UMI; 42: Copyright 1944 Universal Pictures Corp.; 58: Victor R. Boswell, Jr.; 60. Archivo Iconografico, S.A./CORBIS; 64: EM, C/Victor R. Boswell, Jr.; 67: The British Museum; 68: Sando Vannini/CORBIS; 72: Zahi Hawass Library; 74: Zahi Hawass Library; 79: Zahi Hawass Library; 86: Christopher A. Klein; 98: Maltings Partnership, Derby, England; 99: Araldo de Luca/CORBIS; 100: Roger Wood/CORBIS; 103: Zahi Hawass Library; 109: O. Louis Mazzatenta; 110: Araldo de Luca/Archivo White Star; 114-115: Hardy Burton, Griffith Institute, Oxford 1925; 117: Gianni Dagli Orti/CORBIS; 118: Christopher A. Klein; 120: Zahi Hawass Library; 124: Courtesy Mona Mekhemar; 125: Maltings Partnership, Derby, England; 126-127: O. Louis Mazzatenta; 132-133: John Buxton; 143: Araldo de Luca/Archivo White Star; 146-147: Victor R. Boswell, Jr.

Printed in Belgium

To Hathor,

the beautiful lady;

my first and

greatest love.

—ZH

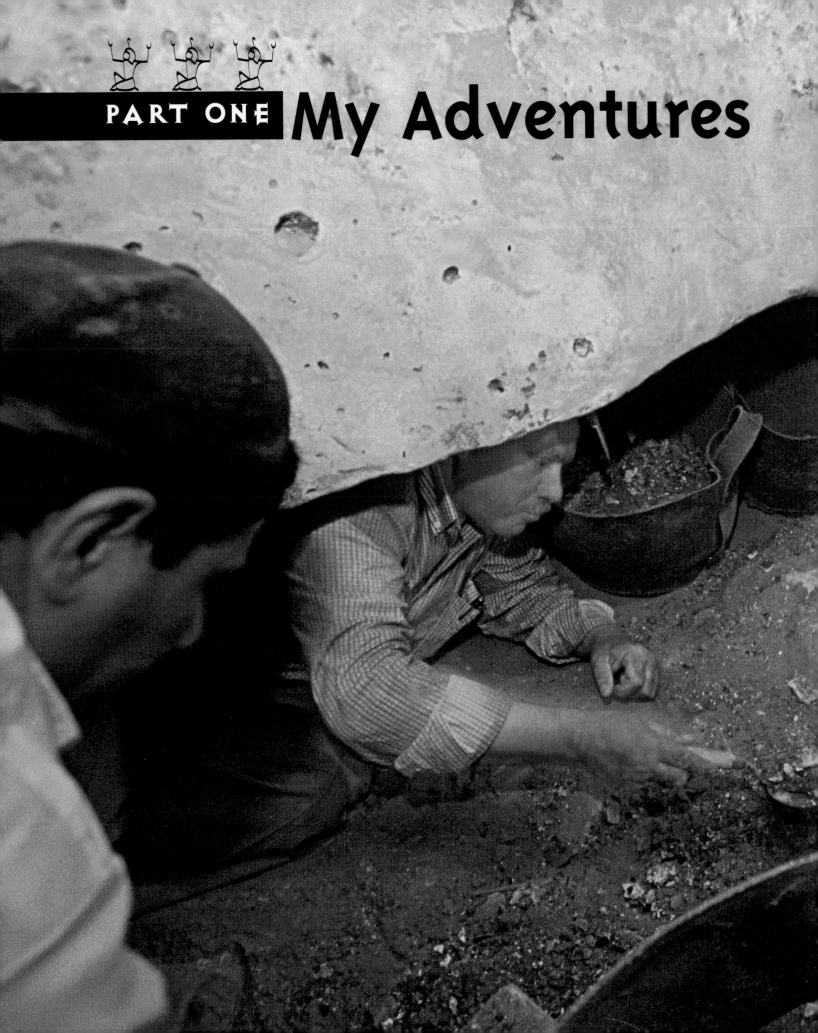

PART ONE My Adventures

Here, my colleagues and I search the ground for artifacts in the tomb of Zed-khonsu-iuf-ankh in the Bahariya Oasis. (I'm at top right in this shot.) Each artifact we find will be carefully recorded. There is nothing like the thrill of finding an ancient piece of the past.

I N T R O D U C T I O N

I LOVE ARCHAEOLOGY. It is my passion, my reason for living. I love to share my adventures with the public, and one of my greatest pleasures is telling my stories to young people around the world. Once I was giving a lecture in Pittsburgh, Pennsylvania, and a young man asked me, "Why do you excavate? Why do you risk your life in dark tunnels and deep shafts? Aren't you afraid of snakes, and poisonous insects, and the curse of the pharaohs?"

Many people believe in the curse of the pharaohs. They think that the souls of the ancient Egyptian dead, once their bodies have been uncovered, will haunt those who disturb their rest. These ancient ghosts are often blamed

Exploring dark tombs requires a bright light and a sense of adventure. Discovering something new about Egypt's past is worth the dangers of exploring the unknown.

 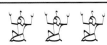

when things go wrong. They are given credit for accidents, illnesses, and even deaths. There are many stories about the curse, and I will tell you some of them in this book.

When this young man asked me about the curse, I thought for a moment. Then I answered that I loved the excitement of exploring the unknown, and that the glimpses of the past that shine through the darkness make all the dangers of archaeology worthwhile. Through my work, I feel connected to my ancient Egyptian ancestors, the gracious and peaceful men and women who built the greatest civilization in the history of the world. Each artifact I touch provides me with a link to these people, and the knowledge that I am often the first person in the modern world to touch something that has been buried for thousands of years gives me a sense of true awe.

I must admit, however, that as a child I was terribly afraid of the dark. If I was sent on an errand after the sun had set, I insisted that my younger brother come with me to keep me safe from the demons that lurked in the shadows. I did not conquer this fear until I was a young archaeologist excavating at the site of Kom Abu Billo in the north of Egypt. We had discovered a Roman well, a relic from the days when Egypt was part of the Roman Empire. The well was more than 70 feet deep. If I looked down into its black depths, my childhood fear would overwhelm me.

In order to get to the bottom of the well, our workmen would tie one man to a rope, lower him down, and then haul him back up when he was ready. Our overseer, Hag Mohammed, a man whom I respected and trusted a great deal, asked me if I wanted to go down. At first I refused. But after ten days of thinking

and worrying, I went to him and told him I was ready. He tied me to the rope, and three men slowly lowered me into the silent depths of the well. I felt my heart beat faster and faster, and I fought against complete panic. I closed my eyes and held tightly to the rope, concentrating on breathing in and out, and then suddenly it was over. I was at the bottom, safe and finally free of my old fear of the dark.

By braving the dark and the unknown, we archaeologists are able to bring the past to life. The objects we find and the settings in which we find them help us tell the story of the past. We can learn who our ancestors were and how they lived. The ancient Egyptians built an extraordinary civilization of great beauty, stability, and peace. By understanding both their successes and their failures, perhaps we can make our own world better.

I AM ONE of the luckiest people in the world, because archaeology is not only my passion, it is my job. I am currently in charge of the Supreme Council of Antiquities in Egypt, the top archaeological job in the country. I spend some of my time excavating, or digging, at important sites around Egypt and discovering wonderful things. I am in charge of the excavations around the pyramids at Giza,

In this picture from my younger days, I am working at the site of Kom Abu Billo, which is in the north of Egypt. It was there that I found my first major artifact and fell completely in love with archaeology.

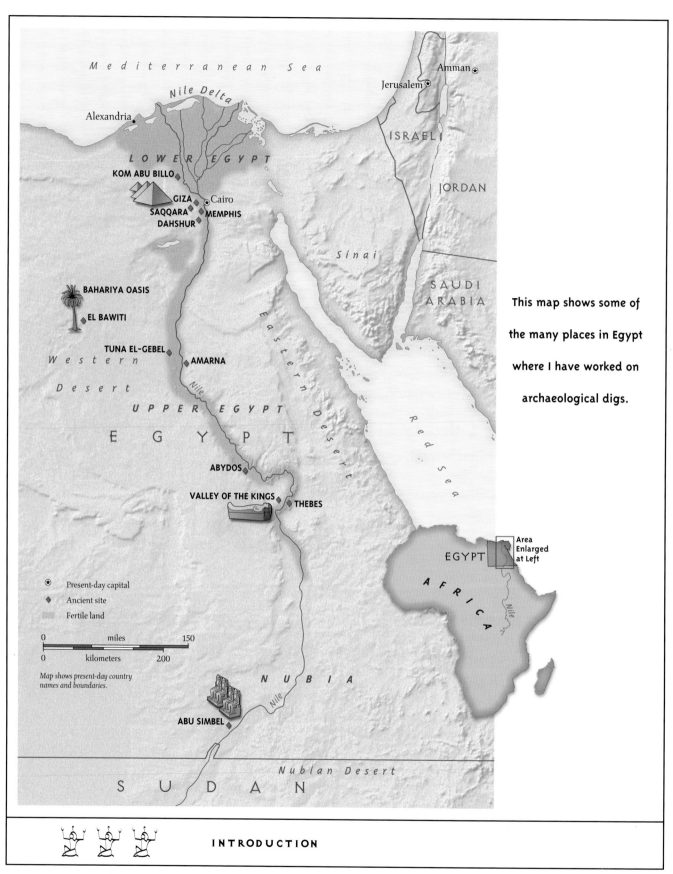

Mediterranean Sea

Nile Delta

Alexandria

Amman

Jerusalem

ISRAEL

JORDAN

LOWER EGYPT

KOM ABU BILLO

GIZA

Cairo

SAQQARA

MEMPHIS

DAHSHUR

Sinai

SAUDI ARABIA

BAHARIYA OASIS

EL BAWITI

TUNA EL-GEBEL

AMARNA

Western

Desert

Nile

UPPER EGYPT

E G Y P T

Eastern Desert

Red Sea

This map shows some of the many places in Egypt where I have worked on archaeological digs.

ABYDOS

VALLEY OF THE KINGS

THEBES

EGYPT

Area Enlarged at Left

A F R I C A

Nile

⊛ Present-day capital

◆ Ancient site

▨ Fertile land

0   miles   150

0   kilometers   200

Map shows present-day country
names and boundaries.

NUBIA

Nile

ABU SIMBEL

Nubian Desert

S U D A N

INTRODUCTION

and in the Valley of the Golden Mummies in the Bahariya Oasis (out in the desert southwest of Cairo), as well as in a number of other places.

I have many other responsibilities. For one thing, I have many people working for me, and I have to make many decisions about the work they do. I am also in charge of giving (or refusing) permission to other archaeologists, both from Egypt and from all over the world, to do archaeological work in Egypt. In addition, I watch over all the Egyptian monuments and make sure they are safe from pollution, thieves, and even tourists (who can do a lot of damage if they are not careful). In my spare time, I have to deal with people who try to make a lot of money by making outrageous claims. Some like to say that aliens from outer space or men from the mythical underwater land called Atlantis built the pyramids. Others tell wild stories about the curse of the pharaohs!

I have found that the best way to deal with these people is by telling everyone the truth about ancient Egypt. This is one of the parts of my job that I like best. The real adventure of archaeology is incredibly exciting, more fun than any of the silly stories people make up. Aliens, men from Atlantis, and crazy mummies sound thrilling, but they are just pretend. I find the true stories of real people who once lived, laughed, and enjoyed life as we do now much more fascinating.

Join me now as I tell you about my own adventures with the magic of archaeology. Together, we will explore the mysterious curse of the pharaohs, and I will tell you of the dangers I have faced as I have discovered tombs, statues, and deep, dark tunnels. So take a deep breath, and come with me on a journey that you will always remember.

May Your Name Live Forever

DO I BELIEVE IN THE CURSE OF THE PHARAOHS? Even if it *does* exist, I certainly do not fear it, although many strange things have happened to me during my years in the field. Let me tell you the story of one of my brushes with the curse. This happened to me in 1992, while I was working in the cemetery where the men and women who built the Giza pyramids are buried. This cemetery is very important because it proves that free Egyptians built the pyramids.

This cemetery was discovered by accident on a hot day in August 1990. At the time I was in charge of the pyramids at Giza, where three of the mightiest kings ever to

The shadow and winged creatures in this ancient Egyptian tomb painting symbolize aspects of one's personality believed to survive in the afterlife.

 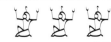

In this picture of the pyramid builders' cemetery, I am sitting on a mud-and-stone tomb belonging to one of the many workers buried at this important site.

rule Egypt were buried. These lie on a high windswept plateau overlooking the modern city of Cairo. I was in my office near the pyramid of the great king Khufu, wearing my usual working outfit of jeans and a denim shirt. I had been thinking, as I often did, about the people who built the pyramids. I decided to go and inspect the Great Pyramid of Khufu, and I reached down to pick up my Indiana Jones hat.

 MAY YOUR NAME LIVE FOREVER

But before I could stand up, the chief of the pyramid guards came rushing in to tell me that a young American woman had been riding in the desert near the pyramids. All of a sudden, her horse had tripped over what seemed to be an ancient wall! Fortunately, the tourist was fine, but the wall looked like it might lead to something exciting. I immediately clapped my hat onto my head, jumped into my car, and drove to the scene of the accident. On the way I hoped and prayed that we had found what I had been seeking for years: the tombs of the pyramid builders.

For a long time, I had been convinced that the tombs of the men and women who built the pyramids lay somewhere at Giza. I had been studying the monuments here for more than ten years, since I was appointed chief archaeologist (my official title was Chief Inspector of Antiquities) in the late 1970s. I had become friends with each of the pyramids, and I had formed a strong bond with the Great Sphinx, the huge rock-cut lion with the head of a king that guards the entrance to the Giza plateau. I had been away for part of this time, earning my Ph.D. in the United States, but my studies had only furthered my resolve to find traces of the people responsible for these spectacular monuments. I was especially keen to prove for once and for all that free Egyptians had built the pyramids, not slaves forced to toil for harsh and cruel masters, and certainly not foreigners, aliens, or men from Atlantis.

When I arrived at the site, which was in the desert not far from the Sphinx, I found that the wall was indeed part of an ancient tomb. It had been buried by the sand for more than 4,000 years, only to be discovered by accident. Our excavations since 1990 have revealed a vast necropolis, or cemetery, at this site.

This bird's-eye view shows the Giza plateau. We found the pyramid builders' cemetery in the cliffs at lower left. At lower right are the remains of what appears to be the workers' town. In the background are the Sphinx, the pyramids, and the city of Cairo.

When I removed the mud bricks from the serdab in Inty-Shedu's tomb, a statue stared back at me! I could see immediately that this was a wonderful example of Old Kingdom art.

The people who were involved in the construction of the Giza pyramids were buried in this necropolis. (The word *necropolis* comes from a Greek word that means "city of the dead.") This is a great discovery. It proves that the pyramids were indeed built by native Egyptians. We know now many of their names, and we know what many of their jobs were. And we can study their bones, which tell us many things about the lives of these important men and women.

HIDDEN STATUES

One of the many wonderful discoveries we made in this cemetery was a group of four beautiful statues belonging to a man named Inty-Shedu. He lived during the Old Kingdom, the age when the pyramids at Giza were built, about 4,500 years ago. Inty-Shedu was the overseer of the sacred boat at the temple of a goddess named Neith. This would have been an important job, since the boat had to be kept ready for the goddess to use whenever she left her temple. While we were excavating Inty-Shedu's tomb, we found what we call a *serdab*. This is an Arabic word that means "cellar." Archaeologists use the term to refer to a small, enclosed chamber without a door.

This serdab, like most, had a small eye-slit near the top. When I looked through this opening, I saw large, expressive eyes looking straight back at me. I knew that we had found a statue. I took photographs of those marvelous eyes through the slit, imagining all the while that a masterpiece of ancient art might lie behind the wall that was in front of me.

The serdab was built of limestone blocks at the bottom, with a wall made of mud bricks above. I began to take down the mud bricks one by one until I could see the face of the statue, which looked like it represented a man of about 45. As I gazed at his face, I felt as if he were alive and had something to tell me.

I told my assistant to seal the tomb entrance behind us to keep out the air, which might damage the ancient stone. Working in the closed tomb, I finished taking down the mud-brick wall. As we continued excavating, we took many photographs, which is an important part of the process of recording our work. Then, with my excavation pick-ax in my right hand and a brush in my left, I began to move a limestone block that was about eight inches high. Through the gap it left, I saw a scene I will never forget as long as I live: Hidden behind the

To my astonishment, I found not one but four statues of Inty-Shedu hidden in the serdab in his tomb. The largest statue portrays him at the time of his death. The smaller figures show other stages of his life.

limestone blocks was not one but four beautiful statues. I was so thrilled by what I saw before me that I dropped the limestone block. It broke in half, and just barely missed my foot.

The discovery of four statues, *in situ* (a fancy way of saying "in their original place"), is very unusual. The statue we had seen first, showing a man with shoulder-length hair and a moustache seated on a chair, was in the center. It was large, about 30 inches tall. To its left were a standing statue and a sitting statue, and to its right was a second standing statue. The statues on the sides were all smaller than the central figure. These four statues were carved out of limestone and painted with bright colors.

The ancient Egyptians were always careful to do things symmetrically, and I found it strange that there would be two statues on one side of the main figure and only one on the other. So I looked carefully, and I saw that there had once been a second statue on the right, but it had been made of wood and had disintegrated into powder.

I felt sad at the loss of the fifth statue, but I began to examine the four extraordinary statues left in front of me. Each was inscribed with the name Inty-Shedu. I knew that they were meant to represent one person at various stages of his life.

STRANGE COINCIDENCES

The discovery of the hidden statues of Inty-Shedu was important news because the statues were masterpieces, beautifully carved and painted by an expert sculptor, and

completely intact. The titles inscribed on the statues told us that Inty-Shedu had been more than a simple workman, and his statues are important because they show him at different stages of his life. The figures are excellent examples of the realistic art of the period. I called our Minister of Culture, Farouk Hosni, and told him what we had found. He set a date to come and see the statues and bring all the newspaper reporters with him.

This is when strange things began to happen. On the day that the announcement was to be made, October 12, 1992, a big earthquake struck Cairo. I was sitting in my office at Giza when I felt the ground shake so hard that some of my books fell off their shelves. I immediately thought about the Sphinx, which is already in great danger of crumbling to pieces, and all our new discoveries, so I ran outside to see if everything was OK. I was very happy to find everything still standing, but we had to postpone the announcement—after the earthquake, the people of Egypt were very upset, and the mood of the country was very gloomy. Everyone had the earthquake on their minds, so this would not have been a good time to announce our discovery.

We set a new date, on a Friday, which is the weekend in Egypt. I usually sleep a little bit late on Fridays then go to a café to write. But that day, because of the announcement about the statues, I got up early. My driver picked me up, and we drove off to the pyramids. (As a government official, I have my own car and someone to drive me wherever I need to go.) I sat in the front seat, reading the paper as I like to do in the morning. Suddenly the sky began to spin, and I fainted—I was having a heart attack!

Not far from my office in Cairo, the Great Sphinx crouches near the pyramids. The king-headed lion was built about 2500 B.C. In this picture it is illuminated by the lights of a sound and light show put on at night for tourists.

I was very lucky because my driver was smart enough to take me right to the hospital, only a few minutes away. I was rushed to the emergency room, where I was given a shot of heart medicine that saved my life. But of course we had to cancel the announcement again. I stayed in the hospital for about two weeks, thinking of Inty-Shedu.

So we never made an official announcement of the statues. Maybe Inty-Shedu was shy and didn't want everyone paying so much attention to him. Some people might say that the earthquake and my heart attack were the result of an ancient curse, to which they like to ascribe all unusual events connected with Egyptology. But if there is a "Curse of Inty-Shedu," it holds no terror for me. It probably saved my life. If I had been home in bed when I had my heart attack, there would have been no one to notice that I needed medical help, and I might well have died!

Inty-Shedu's statues are now in the Cairo Museum, and because they are so near to my heart, I often go and say hello to them. I look at them and remember the day of the discovery, the day of the earthquake, and the day of my heart attack. I smile at them, and they seem to smile back at me.

TREASURING THE PAST

Why do so many people believe in a curse? Why do they want to believe that the ancient Egyptians wish to reach out over thousands of years and do us harm? The greatest desire of the ancient Egyptians was that their names would live forever, granting them immortality. We as archaeologists dedicate our lives to bringing the names of the ancients back to life. We are not plunderers; we are not like the robbers

who ransack tombs in search of treasure, destroying everything in their paths. We do not blindly rip mummies out of their eternal homes, denying the dead their immortality and losing valuable information forever. We are not antiquities thieves, selling bits of the past to people who will hoard them and refuse to share them with the world.

What we do as archaeologists is to study the past, with care and love. We search for remains of the ancients that

A vital part of an archaeologist's job is to keep careful records. Like my colleague above, I make sketches. I also write notes about each find in my diary and take lots of photographs.

X-rays help us look at mummies without damaging them. Here I am inspecting an x-ray of the skull of a mummy I call Mr. X. We learned he had a couple of teeth pulled out!

have been left in place. We treat each grave that we find with respect. We pay attention to the context of each object—exactly where and how it was left. The information that we gather in this way tells us stories about the people who left the objects behind.

When I discover a new tomb, I am always mindful of the person buried inside. I move and touch the mummies I find as little as possible. And I use all of the latest

 MAY YOUR NAME LIVE FOREVER

22

technologies, such as x-rays and CAT scans, so that I can study them without disturbing their delicate bones. Using these tools can give us detailed pictures of the mummies and provide us with lots of information.

By studying ancient bones and artifacts in this way, I can learn so much—the age people were when they died, whether they were sick or healthy, and even what killed them. For example, several of the skeletons from the pyramid builders' cemetery have wounds that suggest that they were hurt or killed during their work on the pyramid site, perhaps by falling blocks. We even know something about the medical care available: One man had his arm amputated and lived for many years afterward.

By studying groups of mummies or tombs or houses, I can find out about families and groups of people, and even the society as a whole. By reading the texts that ancient people have left behind, I can learn about things such as their religious beliefs and how their economy worked.

As an archaeologist, I cause the names of the dead to be remembered, not forgotten. So if there is a curse, it should follow the thieves and robbers who destroy the past, not the scholars who try to preserve it.

The Birth of the Curse

THE CURSE OF THE PHARAOHS became famous all over the world after the discovery of the tomb of Tutankhamun in 1922. This was a remarkable find— one of the few royal tombs from ancient Egypt that had not been stripped of its treasures long ago.

Tutankhamun was only a boy of about eight years old when he became king of Egypt (in about 1300 B.C.) and was still very young when he died. Almost all the royal tombs from the New Kingdom, the era when Tut ruled, had been found, first by robbers and then by archaeologists. But no one had found the tomb of Tutankhamun.

Archaeologist Howard Carter was convinced that Tut's

In the tomb of King Tutankhamun, Howard Carter gazes through the doors of a golden shrine, one of four guarding the young pharaoh's sarcophagus.

tomb lay in the Valley of the Kings, a lonely site in the south of Egypt. This valley (really several connected valleys) lies in the desert across the Nile from the important ancient city of Thebes. It was here that the pharaohs of the New Kingdom (starting about 3,500 years ago) hid their tombs in the rocky cliffs, hoping that robbers wouldn't find them.

No one had believed that Carter and his wealthy sponsor, Lord Carnarvon, would find the tomb, but after years of disappointment, they struck gold. I heard about the discovery firsthand from an eyewitness, a man named Sheikh Aly. I met him when I was a young man of 20 and my hair was still black. He was a weather-beaten old man of 70. He had earned the title of Sheikh, a term of great respect indicating that he was the head of his extended family. At the time, I was working as an inspector of antiquities on the west bank of Thebes. I was supervising an expedition from the University of Pennsylvania that was uncovering the palace of Tutankhamun's grandfather, Amenhotep III. A friend introduced me to Sheikh Aly at his hotel on the west bank of Luxor (the modern name for ancient Thebes), near the place where the ancient kings were buried. We became good friends, and he told me many wonderful stories about the secrets of the pharaohs.

In 1922, Sheikh Aly was just a boy, and the Valley of the Kings was his playground. His family, the Abd el-Rassuls, had lived in the area for as long as anyone could remember. In the 1870s, they had found a large group, or cache, of royal mummies in a secret tomb a few miles from the Valley of the Kings. Around 1000 B.C., a group of Egyptian priests had taken the mummies of all the New Kingdom kings and queens they could find and hidden them in a deep shaft. They

did this to keep them safe from the tomb robbers that constantly roamed the Valley. After finding this shaft, Sheik Aly's family kept it a secret for many years. They only entered it three times, each time removing a few items to sell to feed their children.

In 1881, a member of the family told the authorities about the tomb, and people from the government came and took the mummies away to the Cairo Museum. (The body of Tutankhamun was NOT found in the royal cache.) From then on, different parts of the family fought with one another, and bad things began to happen to them.

Tied by priests more than 3,000 years before Carter discovered Tutankhamun's tomb, this knot of heavy rope held together the doors to one of the shrines in the tomb. The clay seal was intact, proof that grave robbers had not entered the shrine.

Sheikh Aly believed it was because the government had disturbed their ancestors, and this had awakened an ancient curse.

When Carter came to the Valley, the Sheikh's family became part of his team. The Sheikh himself, though very young, helped with the work, and personally witnessed all the important events of the discovery.

CARTER'S GREAT FIND

Many people do not know that Lord Carnarvon had decided to give up the hunt for Tutankhamun at the end of the 1921–22 season, just before the golden tomb was found. After searching for four years (for at least four months each year) and spending vast sums of money, he was tired and fed up. During the summer of 1922, he had called Carter to Highclere, his mansion in England, and told him that he would not pay for any more work. Carter was expecting this and offered to fund the next season out of his own pocket. Lord Carnarvon was impressed with Carter's dedication and agreed to pay for two more months of excavation.

While he was in England, Carter went to a bird shop in London and bought a canary. When he and his canary arrived at the Valley of the Kings in late September 1922, his workmen met him happily. Carter knew enough Arabic to say to the *reis* (the head of the native workers), "I have brought this unique bird." The reis answered that the bird would bring them luck.

Carter and his crew immediately set to work, concentrating in the only area that had not yet been cleared. This was near the tomb of a king named Ramses VI,

who had ruled 200 years after Tutankhamun. In 1917, Carter had found a group of ancient huts where the workmen who built this tomb had lived. He had not wanted to dig under them because the work would have blocked the only access to Ramses VI's tomb, a popular tourist destination in the Valley. But now it was the only place left to look, so he made a careful record of the huts and told his men to dig a trench right through the middle.

Carter spent the next few days inside his tent, wearing long boots, a hat, and a discouraged expression. This year, unlike the others, his men did not see him smile, and they knew that he was incredibly frustrated by his lack of success.

On November 4, 1922, a cool breeze was blowing, and the workmen were singing and chanting as they moved mountains of sand. A little way from the main focus of the work, a young boy with a donkey was bringing large pottery jars full of cool water for the workmen to drink. He took the first jar and dug a hole in the sand in which to set its rounded base. Suddenly his eyes widened as he saw something strange appearing: a step of limestone!

He immediately ran to get Carter, who came to investigate. Carter recognized the step as the beginning of an ancient stairway that could lead down to a tomb. According to Sheikh Aly, he was so excited that he ran back to his tent right away to send a telegram to Lord Carnarvon to tell him to rush back to Egypt. As he entered the tent, he saw a cobra eating his canary! This strange and disturbing occurrence was said to be the beginning of the "Curse of Tutankhamun."

Carter was too excited, however, to dwell on the bird's death. He and his crew cleared most of the stairway and found that it did indeed lead to the blocked doorway of a tomb. Stamped many times into the plaster that covered this door-way were the seals of the ancient necropolis guards. These told Carter that he had found a royal tomb. He was sure that he had discovered Tutankhamun.

"WONDERFUL THINGS!"

On November 23, 1922, Carnarvon and his daughter, Lady Evelyn Herbert, along with the Egyptian crew, watched as the rest of the debris was cleared and the name of Tutankhamun found for the first time (on several of the necropolis seals stamped onto the plaster near the bottom of the doorway). At the top left-hand corner of the doorway, Carter could see that the plaster had been broken through twice and then resealed in antiquity by the necropolis guards, so he knew that the tomb had been entered after the king was put to rest. But he pushed ahead, order-ing the men to remove the plaster blocking from the doorway and then clear the rubble from the downward-sloping passageway that lay before them. This led to another blocked doorway, which had also been sealed and resealed thousands of years ago.

On November 26, 1922, Carter made a small hole in the plaster blocking, just big enough for a candle. He peered in and was struck speechless by what he saw before him. Lord Carnarvon, who was standing behind him, asked impatiently, "Can you see anything?" Carter replied, "Wonderful things!" Later, he reported that he saw, "strange animals, statues, and gold—everywhere the glint of gold."

The world watched in awe over the course of the next decade as a steady stream of magnificent artifacts made of precious metals, native and imported woods,

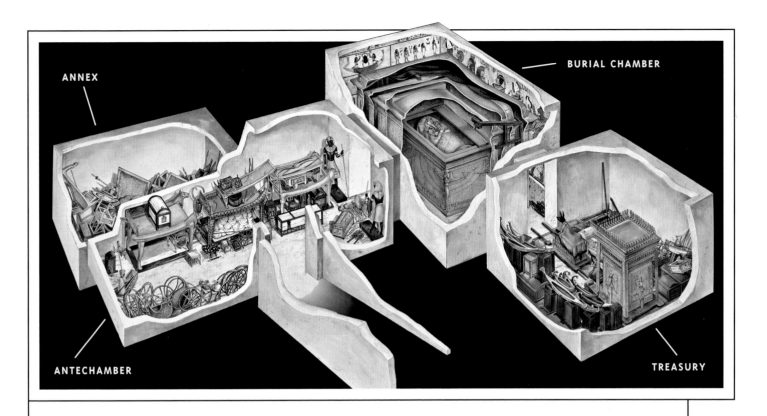

ANNEX

BURIAL CHAMBER

ANTECHAMBER

TREASURY

fabulous cloth, and stone carved into fantastic shapes poured from the packed chambers of Tutankhamun's tomb. As Carter had suspected, ancient robbers had indeed penetrated the secret burial, but they had been caught before they could take more than a fraction of its contents. It was a spectacular discovery—the almost-intact tomb of an ancient Egyptian pharaoh, filled with more than 5,000 objects: the clothes, jewelry, furniture, weapons, chariots, and ceremonial equipment that the king had used during his lifetime and the many items he would need for his afterlife. Every piece tells us something about the boy-king's life: the love between him and his wife

Tutankhamun's tomb had four rooms. Carter called the first room the antechamber. Behind it was the annex, which held more than 2,000 everyday objects. The burial chamber held four nesting shrines, with Tut's coffin at center. The riches-filled fourth room was dubbed the treasury.

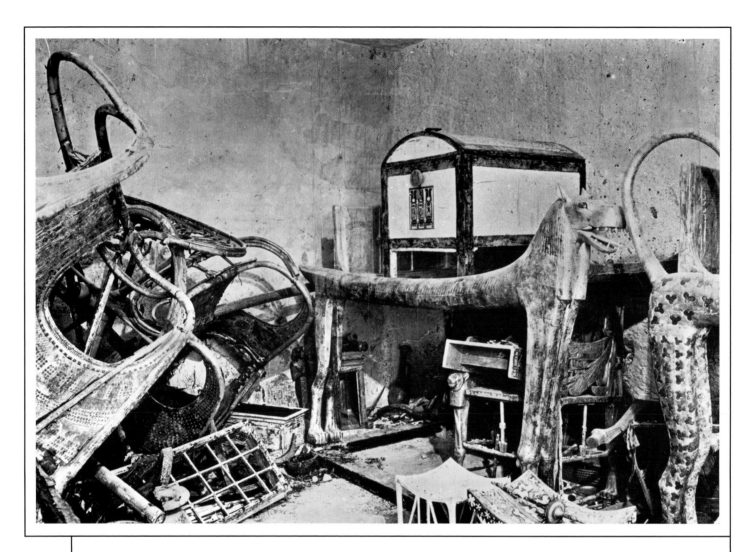

Their first view of the antechamber in Tutankhamun's tomb must have dazzled Carter and Lord Carnarvon. Among the clutter were three gilded beds and four dismantled chariots.

(who was also his half-sister), his enjoyment of hunting, his growth from a child to a young man, and his changing religious beliefs. His mummified body was still there, lying at rest in a nest of golden coffins. The tomb held treasures beyond the imagination, and it also contained a wealth of information, giving us a glittering glimpse into the past.

The news of Tut's discovery grabbed the attention of the whole world, and Carter and his team were soon

 THE BIRTH OF THE CURSE

overrun by people wanting to see the excavations. The visitors took a toll: Work had to slow down or stop, and every guest left a legacy of minor destruction. In order to keep the excavation team from being inundated by hundreds of reporters, Lord Carnarvon sold exclusive rights to the story to the London *Times*. This caused a great deal of trouble with the Egyptian government—Carter and Carnarvon acted as though the tomb was in England, rather than Egypt, and they treated the Egyptian officials and journalists as if they were foreigners in their own land! There is even evidence that Carter and Carnarvon stole some artifacts from the tomb.

THE LEGEND BEGINS

In late February 1923, Lord Carnarvon was bitten by a mosquito. The next day, he cut open the bite while shaving and developed a severe infection. Then Carnarvon contracted pneumonia. He died on April 5, 1923, only five months after the discovery of the tomb. The death of Lord Carnarvon triggered a spate of stories about the "Curse of the Pharaohs," many of them from disgruntled journalists.

Covered in gold, this hippopotamus head topped a post of one of the large wooden beds found in the antechamber of Tutankhamun's tomb. Its teeth are made of ivory.

innermost coffin was made of solid gold. It contained his mummy.

Howard Carter (right) walks with Lord Carnarvon in the Valley of the Kings. Carnarvon financed the search for Tutankhamun's tomb. His death five months after Tut was found gave rise to stories about the curse of the pharaohs.

These journalists were tired of constantly being scooped by the London *Times*, and the legend of the curse grew.

The curse of the pharaohs, also known as the curse of the mummy, was not entirely new. It seems to have been invented in 1827, when a young English novelist named Jane Webb Louden wrote a futuristic novel called *The Mummy*. In the book, a young scholar named Edric fights against an angry mummy who has come back to life. Webb's example was followed in 1869 by Louisa May Alcott, author of *Little Women*, who wrote a short story called "Lost in a Pyramid; or, The Mummy's Curse." In this story, the hero uses part of a mummified priestess as a torch to light his way into the interior of a pyramid. There he finds a golden box containing three oddly shaped seeds. He takes the box back to America, where his fiancée plants the strange seeds. She wears the flowers that grow from them at their wedding, and their odor sends her into a coma.

But these and other similar stories were clearly science fiction or fantasy, like tales of Dracula or Frankenstein. Back when Tutankhamun's tomb was found, there were journalists and other people—as now—who wanted to catch people's attention in order to build up their own

Hearse With Lord Westbury's Body Kills Boy; Museum Death Also Laid to 'Pharaohs' Curse'

LONDON, Feb. 25 (Æ).—Two more deaths which the superstitious were inclined to associate with the opening of Tut-ankh-Amen's tomb were attracting attention here today.

As a hearse was bearing the body of the late Lord Westbury to a crematorium today, it knocked down and killed an 8-year-old boy, Joseph Greer. Lord Westbury had committed suicide on Saturday and his act was ascribed by many to the alleged curse of the Pharaohs. His son, Richard Bethell, died last November after serving as secretary to Howard Carter, who opened the tomb.

The other death was that of Edgar Steele, 57, a worker in the British Museum who had cared for some of the relics from the tombs of Luxor.

He died after an operation for an internal trouble.

An official of the museum scouted the suggestion that there was anything sinister in Steele's death, however, and Mr. Carter has declared that the curse is nothing but a myth.

The museum official remarked that thousands of people had been indirectly connected with the Tut-ankh-Amen relics and that there was no record of any overwhelming outbreak of mortality.

"I've handled Egyptian relics myself many times, for years, and I'm still as well as ever," he said.

The Pharaohs' curse, legend has it, doomed to a quick death any one molesting the tombs of the ancient Egyptian rulers.

---

egos and make money. They reported all sorts of stories and spread rumors like wildfire—including speculations that an ancient curse had been awakened when Tutankhamun's burial chamber was opened.

While Carnarvon lay ill with pneumonia at the Shepheard's Hotel in Cairo, curse stories were spread by a novelist named Marie Corelli. She claimed that she possessed a rare book in Arabic entitled *The Egyptian History*

Seven years after the discovery of Tut's tomb, tales of the legendary curse of the pharaohs were still going strong, as this February 26, 1930, article from the *New York Times* shows.

THE BIRTH OF THE CURSE

of the Pyramids, which supposedly stated: "...the most dire punishment follows any rash intruder into a sealed tomb..." and "...secret poisons [are] enclosed in boxes in such wise that those who touch them shall not know how they come to suffer." She also hinted that something more sinister than a mosquito bite had made Lord Carnarvon sick.

Many other stories of mysterious events supposedly related to the curse appeared and spread:

* One journalist reported that as Lord Carnarvon lay dying on his hotel bed in Cairo, the lights flashed on and off many times, and he began speaking in a language that no one could understand.

* Carnarvon's son, Lord Portchester, repeated in many speeches that his father's favorite dog, Susie, had howled and keeled over dead at the same moment that Lord Carnarvon died.

* Another journalist claimed that the mosquito bite on Carnarvon's cheek was in the same place as a scar on Tutankhamun's face.

* The press published a picture of the golden shrine that housed the canopic jars (jars containing the internal organs of the king that had been removed, carefully wrapped, and placed into a series of nested containers), and reported that the inscription on the outside of the shrine read: "For those who enter the sacred tomb, the wings of death will visit them quickly."

* The inscription on a mud brick that was found in front of a statue of the god Anubis was "translated" and published as follows: "I will kill all of those who cross this threshold into the sacred precincts of the royal king..."

Other deaths were ascribed to the curse:

* Lord Carnarvon's younger brother, Aubrey Herbert, died suddenly in September 1923.

* A. C. Mace, an Egyptologist who worked closely with Carter to record and empty the tomb, died before the work was finished.

* An x-ray expert on his way to examine the mummy of the boy king died before he reached Egypt.

* Jay Gould, an American railroad magnate, caught a cold on his visit to the tomb. This developed into the pneumonia from which he died.

* A French Egyptologist named Georges Benedite fell while exploring the tomb and died later from his injuries.

* An Egyptian prince was murdered by his jealous wife in a London hotel. The press reported that the soul of an Egyptian princess had escaped from the tomb, possessed the wife, and killed the husband!

Any death connected with Egypt or its antiquities in any way (even from before the discovery of Tut's tomb) was said to be caused by the curse. For example, some believers suggested that the death in 1832 of Jean-François Champollion, the man who first deciphered Egyptian hieroglyphs, was due to the curse.

Another death linked retroactively to the curse of the mummies occurred in the late 19th century, when two beautiful statues were found at a site called Meidum. These were from the reign of Khufu, builder of the Great Pyramid. He had declared that there could be statues only of kings and gods, that private people could no longer place statues of themselves in their tombs. But a very

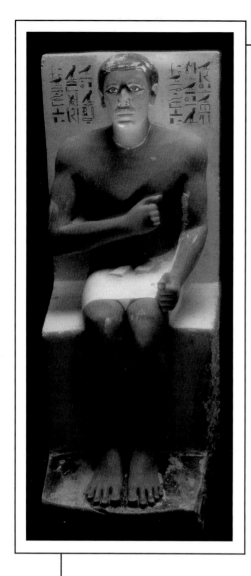

powerful man named Rahotep, who was a close relative of the king and a high official in the government, hid statues of himself and his wife Nofret inside his tomb chapel and bricked up the entrance. In 1871, the French Egyptologist Auguste Mariette sent a team to open this tomb. The first workman to enter saw the incredibly life-like images, fully painted in glorious color, their eyes gleaming with inlaid crystal. Some sources report that he screamed and fell over dead of a heart attack.

THE LEGEND LIVES ON

Stories of the curse of the pharaohs were revived in the 1970s, when selected treasures from Tutankhamun's tomb went on tour around the world. The man who headed the Egyptian Antiquities Organization at the time was Mohammed Mahdy. One day in 1977, he signed a contract allowing 50 artifacts from Tut's tomb to travel to the United States and London. That afternoon as he left his office at the Cairo Museum, he was hit by a car and killed!

A German journalist named Phillip Vandenburg wrote a popular book called *The Curse of the Pharaohs*. As part of his research, he interviewed Dr. Gamal Mehrez, who

succeeded Dr. Mahdy as head of the Egyptian Antiquities Organization, about the curse. When asked if he believed in the curse, Dr. Mehrez said, "I've been working as an archaeologist for the last thirty years, I've discovered temples, tombs, and mummies, and I'm still healthy." The next day, he died of a heart attack.

This same writer also claimed that there had been a tablet in Tut's tomb inscribed: "Death will slay with his wings whoever disturbs the peace of the pharaoh." No one else has ever mentioned seeing this tablet, and, according to Mr. Vandenburg, it was lost long ago.

Talk of the curse continues. I spent seven years in Philadelphia during the 1980s, studying for my doctorate at the University of Pennsylvania. I was amazed by the things I saw and heard while I was in America. For example, one morning I read in the paper that an American man who worked in the tourism business had killed his wife. The defense claimed that this murder had not been the man's fault, that he was under the influence of the curse: A *ushabti*—a funerary statuette he had bought in Egypt—had forced him to stab his wife to death.

Hollywood has been making silly movies for years about mummies and curses. Two recent movies, *The*

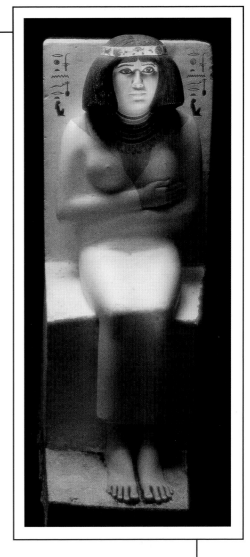

This statue portrays Nofret, wife of Rahotep (opposite). Egyptians of the time believed that such statues needed to be lifelike so that the spirits of the dead would recognize them.

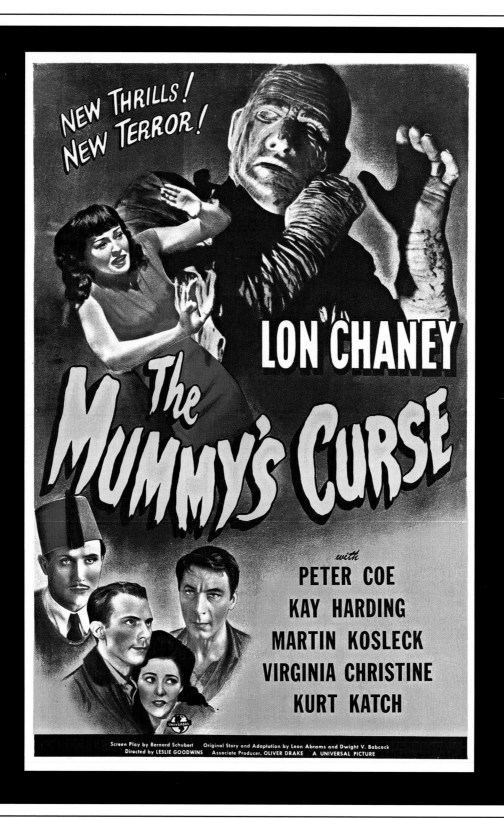

Mummy and *The Mummy Returns*, are especially ridiculous. I recently gave a lecture to a group of children, and they all wanted to know about the flesh-eating scarabs that eat a man in the first movie! (Scarab beetles do NOT eat people.)

American tabloid newspapers are also guilty of a lot of silliness. One day I read in one of these that AIDS had come to the United States because of the curse, that an ancient Egyptian priestess had been infected with this disease. Outraged, I sat down to write a letter to the editor objecting to this lie. Later I found out that it was not unusual for these sorts of publications to write stories like this one. No one is supposed to believe them, but of course many people do.

I was touched personally by people's belief in the curse once when I was giving a lecture in Norristown, Pennsylvania. A woman in the audience stood and said, "I am a healthy young woman, and until recently I had never been ill and had never even seen a doctor. I went to visit Egypt two months ago and touched a statue at the museum. When I came back, I got sick."

But my biggest surprise came when Mayor Bradley came from Los Angeles to visit Egypt several years ago, and I took him on a tour of the pyramids. At the time, we were working on a major restoration of the Sphinx. The mayor wanted to climb up on the paw of the Sphinx, but I teased him by saying that any official who climbed on the paw of the Sphinx would lose his job. Even though he didn't climb up on the paw, the next month Bradley lost the election and his job as mayor of Los Angeles!

For years, Hollywood has been making horror movies—such as the one advertised in this poster—about evil curses and crazy mummies brought back to life.

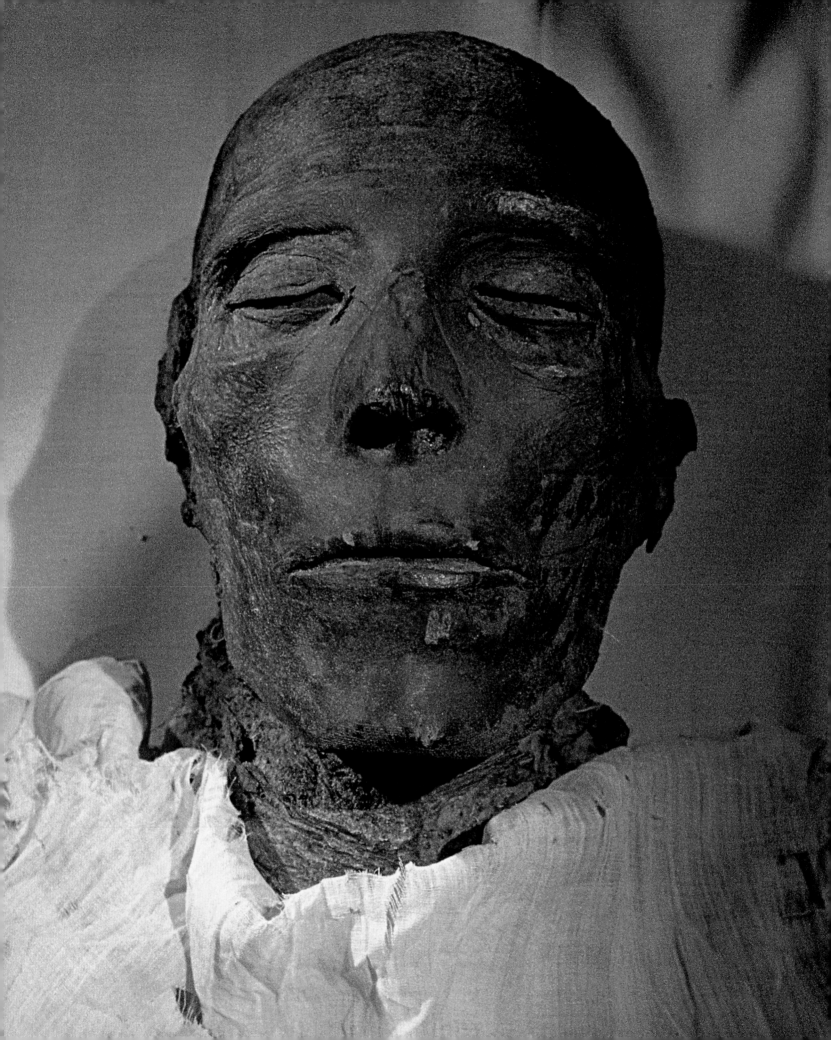

Real Egyptian Curses

IS THERE A CURSE OF THE PHARAOHS? Did the ancient Egyptians believe in curses and magic? The answer to the second question, at least, is yes. The ancient Egyptians often inscribed threatening curses on the walls and doorways of their tombs. I recently found two of these in the tomb chapel of an Old Kingdom (about 2686–2160 B.C.) official named Petety. Petety and his wife Nesy-Sokar built a large, beautifully decorated tomb of mud brick and limestone in the Cemetery of the Pyramid Builders at Giza. (That's the same place where we discovered the tomb of Inty-Shedu.) There are two slightly different curse inscriptions, one for Petety and one for Nesy-Sokar, inscribed on the sides of a

Besides inscribing curses on their tombs, Egyptians took other steps to protect their eternal rest. The tomb of Seti I (left) was concealed to fool looters.

doorway leading into the innermost chamber of the chapel. The curses warn people not to damage the sacred monument:

> Oh, all people who enter this tomb,
>
> Who will make evil against this tomb, and destroy it:
>
> May the crocodile be against them on water,
>
> And snakes against them on land.
>
> May the hippopotamus be against them on water,
>
> The scorpion against them on land.

Most curse inscriptions come from nonroyal tombs of the Old Kingdom. In general, these inscriptions ask everyone who passes by to say some prayers for the tomb owner, for which they will be rewarded. But then they warn that anyone who does any evil to the tomb will be subject to all sorts of punishments. My favorite is "I [the tomb owner] will wring his neck like a goose." Other threats are that the evildoer will be haunted on earth, that his descendents will be wiped out (so there will be no one to care for his tomb), and that he will be judged by the great god. I have seen similar curses in tombs from the Middle Kingdom (about 2055–1650 B.C.).

Although I had read about such curses and had seen them on tombs excavated long ago, Petety's was the first one that I found myself. To add to my excitement, Petety and Nesy-Sokar's tomb had not been entered for thousands of years. I have always been committed to disturbing the tombs I find as little as possible, while extracting as much information as I can. This curse strengthened my resolve to

A visitor studies ancient graffiti at the entrance to the tomb of Ramses XI in the Valley of the Kings. Never finished, the tomb was probably the last built at the site.

preserve every aspect of the sites I excavate. When I find a skeleton or mummy, my team and I examine it, and I have it x-rayed (which tells us a lot but does no damage). But then I put the body back inside the tomb, so the man or woman can continue his or her eternal rest undisturbed.

When I was a young archaeologist, my first posting was at the site of Tuna el-Gebel in Middle Egypt, out in the middle of nowhere. When I was ordered to go to this site, I

refused at first, because I couldn't imagine living in the desert, far away from my friends and family. The man who was head of the Antiquities Service at the time was very angry, and I was almost banned forever from the department forever! But eventually I went, in 1969, and it was there that my love affair with archaeology began. I had lots of time to myself to explore the monuments—tombs, temples, and other interesting antiquities—and I began to learn firsthand about the world of the ancient Egyptians.

One of the most interesting tombs at Tuna el-Gebel was built for a man named Petosiris, who lived in about 300 B.C. At the time, the Greek descendents of the family of Alexander the Great ruled Egypt. This tomb shows a remarkable blending of the Greek and Egyptian traditions. The reliefs in the tomb are in Greek style, and the people wear Greek clothing, but the themes and the tomb itself are Egyptian. And Petosiris, following the Egyptian tradition, put a curse inscription in his tomb that begs visitors to perform the proper rites rather than commit acts of sacrilege. He threatens anyone who does him harm with dire punishments, and warns that if they are not punished on earth, they will be judged after death.

A statue of Mereruka, an Old Kingdom official, stands in a false doorway in his Saqqara tomb. Gifts for his use in the afterlife were left in front of his statue.

There is no doubt that the ancient Egyptians believed in an afterlife, an eternal existence beyond the grave. It was very important to them that their bodies be preserved (as a mummy if they were wealthy enough to afford it) and that they have all the things they would need to travel safely to the next world and live there happily.

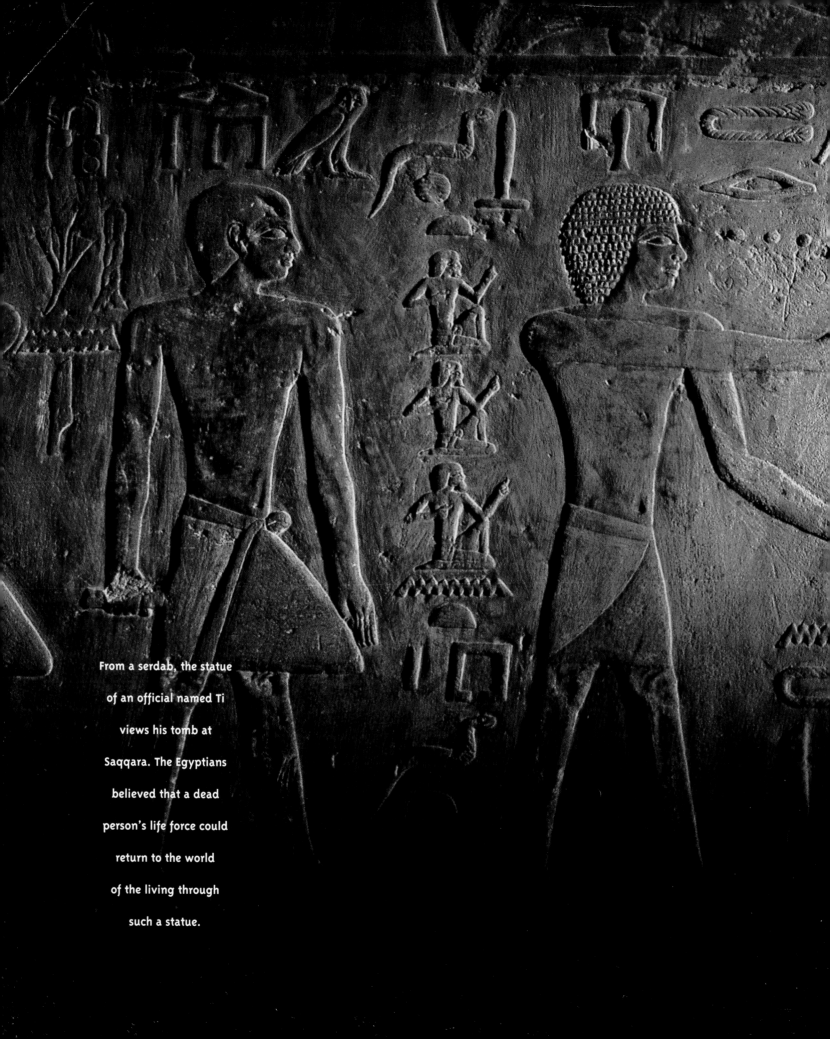

From a serdab, the statue
of an official named Ti
views his tomb at
Saqqara. The Egyptians
believed that a dead
person's life force could
return to the world
of the living through
such a statue.

Here a member of my team is removing rubble from hieroglyphs inscribed on the tomb of a royal doctor named Qar. The inscription reads, "Physician of the Palace, Qar."

They also believed that the dead still had power in this world. People even wrote letters to their dead relatives and left them in their tomb chapels, asking them for help. One woman, for example, wrote to her dead husband asking him to make sure their servant girl got well again. Another such letter is from a husband to his dead wife. He asks her why she has left him and complains about how unhappy he is without her.

REAL EGYPTIAN CURSES

GRAVE ROBBERS

Tomb robbery has existed since the earliest days of Egypt. Everyone knew that curse inscriptions alone were not enough to stop thieves, no matter how horrible the threats. So builders also tried to hide the tombs. Burials were often made at the bottom of shafts, which were then filled in with rocks and rubble. The tomb of a royal doctor named Qar,

I am examining the wall decoration in the chapel of Qar's tomb. Although the shaft beneath this chapel was 60 feet deep, thieves still managed to find their way into the burial chamber.

These 4,300-year-old bronze surgical tools from Qar's tomb are the oldest ever found in Egypt. I believe they were used for cutting and sewing, perhaps even for brain surgery.

which I discovered recently at Saqqara (not far from Giza), had a burial shaft that was 60 feet deep!

Even the deepest shafts, however, did not discourage tomb robbers. Although Qar's tomb still contained objects of great interest to archaeologists—such as beautiful pottery jars and, most astonishingly, the good doctor's surgical tools—ancient thieves had stolen many things from it. Here, as in many other tombs, they simply dug

down through the rubble. In some cases the looters started from the bottom of one shaft and dug tunnels from one shaft to another.

The accuracy with which some of these tunnels were aimed tells us that the thieves knew exactly where they were going. Many of the robbers were probably the same men who had dug the tombs in the first place! We even know of tombs that were robbed before they were sealed. The only people who could have done this were the priests who were supposed to be guarding them.

ROYAL TOMBS

Royal tombs were not inscribed with curses. They relied on a different kind of protection. In the Old Kingdom, the kings were buried inside great pyramids, where they were watched over night and day by priests and guards. The entrances and inside corridors were blocked with great slabs of granite, which is a very hard stone. This gave them more protection, because it is very hard to make a tunnel through a granite block.

I can imagine the moment when the ancient priests placed the mummy of the king inside his sarcophagus (a

The robbers who looted Qar's tomb left behind these offering plates. Artifacts such as these give us a fascinating glimpse of life in ancient Egypt.

word for a fancy coffin) and left the burial chamber one by one. The last priest to leave the chamber would have given the order to let down the slab to seal the king into his resting place for eternity. As I write, I can hear the sound of the heavy granite block sliding into place, falling with a crash that echoes down the corridor of time.

Even the main entrance to the pyramid was completely blocked so that no one could find its location. In the ninth century A.D., Caliph Al-Mamun, son of Harun al-Rashid, the caliph immortalized in the *Thousand and One Nights*, came with his soldiers to the Great Pyramid of Khufu to search for the treasure believed to be buried inside. They looked and looked, but could not find the hidden passageway. So they dug a new entrance (missing the real one by only a few feet), which people today still use to visit Khufu's final resting place.

I've learned firsthand how difficult it can be to get into a tomb. Several years ago, for example, I had the experience of being the first person in modern times to enter the pyramid of one of the queens of Menkaure, the builder of the Third Pyramid at Giza. I did this on live TV.

This statute portrays King Menkaure, builder of the Third Pyramid at Giza. On his right is the goddess Hathor; on his left is the guardian goddess of an upper Egyptian province.

The descending passageway was only about a foot wide and 60 feet long, and it was extremely difficult to navigate. When I got to the entrance to the burial chamber, I found it blocked by a huge granite slab. There was a gap of only about eight inches between the floor and the edge of the slab. I tried to slide underneath, and right there on worldwide television, I got stuck! I was afraid I

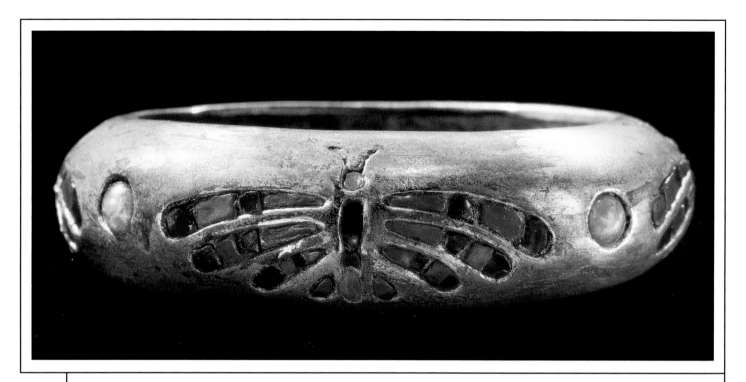

Many treasures—including this beautiful golden bracelet—were discovered in the tomb of Queen Hetepheres in 1925, along with a great mystery: Although the queen's sarcophagus was there, her mummy was nowhere to be found.

would never get out. My friends who watched the program told me later that they could hardly breathe, they were so frightened for me. The TV host, who was behind me, had to take the camera off my back so I could squeeze through.

We already knew that the pyramid had been robbed in ancient times, but it was still an enormous thrill to enter the long-abandoned tomb of Menkaure's queen. As I left the burial chamber again and started back up the narrow passageway to the entrance, I slipped and slid back down the passageway. I had quite a hard time getting back out of the pyramid.

So you see, the ancient builders did everything that

they could to protect their tombs. They made things as difficult as they could for tomb robbers AND archaeologists.

Unfortunately, these precautions were not enough, and all of the Old Kingdom pyramids were emptied of their treasures. We know that the tomb of at least one queen, Hetepheres, was robbed thousands of years ago. A secret shaft in the shadow of the Great Pyramid was found by archaeologists at Giza in 1925. Inside was most of her funerary equipment—the things that were buried with her, which included some wonderful treasures. But the archaeologists who found her tomb also discovered a great mystery. Even though the chamber at the bottom of the shaft contained her jewelry, her furniture, her coffin, and even her canopic box (which contained her inner organs, removed when she was mummified), her body was missing.

I believe that Hetepheres was originally buried in one of the small pyramids nearby. Sometime after she was buried, maybe right away or maybe several hundred years later, robbers broke into her tomb, and they stole or destroyed her mummy. The thieves were probably caught before they could steal everything else. The priests in charge of the Giza plateau at the time must have taken everything that remained and put it into this secret shaft so that no one would find it. And it worked. The shaft remained hidden for more than 3,000 years, until archaeologists found it. Now the beautiful treasures of Hetepheres are safe in the Cairo Museum, where anyone can enjoy them and learn from them. The priests, with help from archaeologists, succeeded in making Hetepheres's name live forever.

Carved from
granite, this statue
portrays King
Amenemhet III
in the form of a
sphinx—a symbol of
power and strength.

The government of Egypt fell apart at the end of the Old Kingdom (in about 2160 B.C.). Without strong kings in charge, there was no one to guard the pyramids, no one to take care of kings who had been buried hundreds of years before. It was as it would be if the government founded in the United States in 1776 no longer ran the country—there would be no one to take care of the Liberty Bell, the Washington Monument, or the Lincoln Memorial. After the Old Kingdom fell, rulers from different cities tried to take over Egypt. They fought one other, each trying to gain power for themselves. They did not care about the kings who had come before them, and they were not buried in pyramids themselves.

Once the country was reunited (in about 2055 B.C., after a hundred years of disorder), the monarchs of the Middle Kingdom went back to burial in pyramids. But the Middle Kingdom rulers had learned from the past.

They knew that the huge sealed pyramids were not enough to protect the royal mummies and their treasures. So these kings hid their treasures and their mummies in elaborate labyrinths, or mazes, that were constructed underneath the pyramids. Complete with dead-end corridors and false burial chambers, these were intended to conceal the way to the real burial chambers.

I recently visited an archaeologist named Dieter Arnold, who was excavating under the pyramid of Amenemhet III at Dahshur. This king lived during the Middle Kingdom, about 3,200 years ago. I entered this pyramid, known as the Black Pyramid, and found myself in a maze of corridors. It was confusing and even frightening. I felt that I could lose my way completely and not be able to find my way back out if I wasn't careful. But even clever mazes like this one could not keep out determined thieves, and the Middle Kingdom pyramids, too, were eventually robbed. Once again, they were safe only as long as the priests and guards did their duty. When the Middle Kingdom fell and the country again entered into a period of chaos (about 1650 B.C.), tomb robbers broke into the pyramids, found their way through the mazes into the burial chambers, and stripped them of their contents.

DISTURBING THE DEAD

In the New Kingdom, which began about 1550 B.C., the kings tried a new tactic. Instead of building huge, highly visible tombs, they constructed mortuary temples (places where priests would perform rituals for their cults) out in the open, but they hid their actual tombs in the crevices and crannies of the Valley of the Kings.

Two pyramids loom
above the desert sands at
Dahshur. At left is the
so-called Bent Pyramid of
King Snerfu. At right are
the crumbling remains of
Amenemhet III's Black
Pyramid, which contains
a very confusing maze
of corridors.

(King Tutankhamun ruled during the New Kingdom, and the Valley of the Kings is where Carter found his tomb.) The first king to do this was Tuthmosis I, whose architect, Ineni, bragged in inscriptions in his own tomb that he had supervised the carving of his royal master's treasure chambers in secret, "…alone, no one seeing, no one hearing." We must wonder what happened to the workmen who did the actual digging!

The entrances to the royal tombs were small and inconspicuous, and the entrance passages were often left undecorated so that they looked unfinished and unused. In many tombs, the final chamber was a dummy, or fake. The real tomb continued under its floor. Just before the antechamber (the last room before the burial chamber) was a deep well with a false wall, decorated to look intact, on the other side. But in the end, not even these elaborate deceptions provided protection. The glittering gold and precious oils and gems buried with the kings were too tempting, and the thieves were too greedy and too clever to give up the search. Perhaps they themselves, or their cousins or friends, had helped carve the tombs.

Valuable treasures, such as this golden pendant found in the tomb of Princess Khnumet, have long tempted—and continue to tempt—thieves to rob tombs.

Perhaps some of the architects took bribes. Perhaps some of the thieves were just lucky, or persistent. We don't know exactly how they did it, but robbers eventually found their way into almost all of the royal tombs.

We know, for example, that the tomb of Tuthmosis IV was robbed within a few years of his death. Even the tomb of King Tut was broken into only a few days after his funeral. We think that the thieves heard the necropolis

Many pharaohs of the New Kingdom, including King Tutankhamun, were buried in the Valley of the Kings. Thieves found their way into nearly all of the royal tombs.

police coming—they were probably smart and careful enough to post a lookout, since they knew they would be in terrible trouble if they were caught. At any rate, some of the thieves escaped, taking metals and precious oils with them. When the guards came, they resealed the tomb.

There are even texts that tell us about ancient tomb robbers who were caught in the act. In one, a judge in the courtroom asked the thief, "Why did you steal from the tomb of Pharaoh?" The thief, who clearly did not believe in

 **REAL EGYPTIAN CURSES**

a curse, replied, "Everyone says that the Pharaoh is a god, why didn't he stop me?"

Another group of texts tells the story of a struggle between Paser, the honest mayor of the East Bank of Thebes, and Pawera, the corrupt mayor of the West Bank. Pawera was supposed to be guarding the Valley of the Kings and the nearby areas where queens, nobles, and officials were buried. But instead, he and his chief of police were breaking into the royal tombs and stealing

This papyrus from around 1100 B.C. tells a story of tomb robbery in the Valley of the Kings. The thieves were corrupt officials—including a chief of police—who were supposed to be guarding the sacred tombs.

REAL EGYPTIAN CURSES

their treasures. They kept their secret by bribing anyone who might give them trouble.

Paser heard about the thefts and reported them to the vizier, who was the most powerful man in the land after the pharaoh. The vizier appointed a committee to investigate, but all of the men on it were dishonest. They lied to the vizier, telling him that all of the tombs were still intact.

Paser wrote again to the Pharaoh, telling him that the committee had been bribed. This time the king found men who were honest and loyal to investigate the matter. They were shocked to find many of the royal tombs stripped of their treasures. The thieves were caught, tortured, and found guilty in a court of law, punished not by the curse of the dead but by the command of the living. We know that the thieves were put to death in some gruesome way, although we don't know the details.

So you see, if there is an age-old curse that punishes those who disturb the pharaohs' rest (which I find highly unlikely), it was not powerful enough to scare away the ancient grave robbers. Indeed, it is clear from these ancient texts that such thieves feared only the living, not the dead.

This tomb painting, which dates to the sixth or seventh century B.C., features a god holding a spear. He may look fierce, but it is unlikely that he frightened away looters.

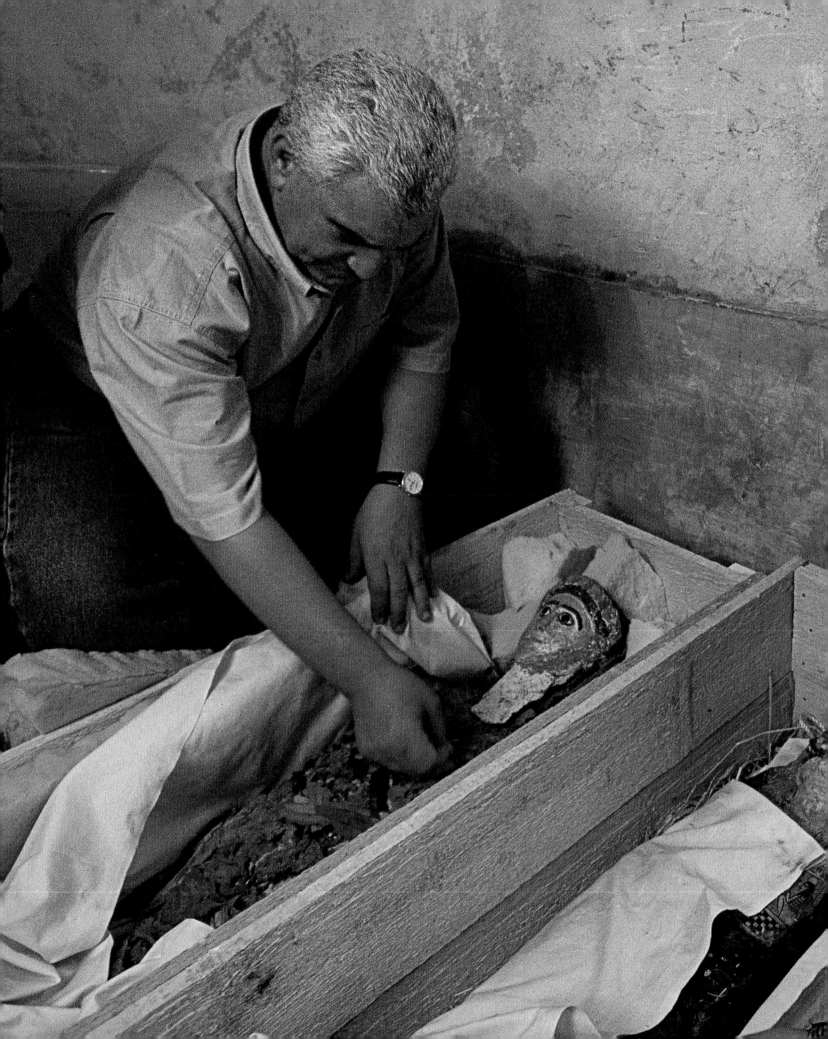

My Real-Life Brushes with the Curse

LIKE THE TOMB ROBBERS OF LONG AGO, I do not fear the curse of the pharaohs. But I myself have had several brushes with the magic of ancient Egypt, besides the episode with Inty-Shedu, which I told you about earlier.

I had my first experience with this magic when I was a young archaeologist working at the site of Kom Abu Billo, the place where I conquered my fear of the dark. Kom Abu Billo lies in the delta, which is the fan-shaped area of northern Egypt where the Nile River branches out as it enters the sea. I spent six years there, starting in 1969, and it was a very exciting time for me. It was there that I found my first major artifact, a

Before taking him to the museum, I look at the little boy mummy from the Valley of the Golden Mummies. I did not know then that I would see him again—in my dreams.

This is the statuette I found when I was a young archaeologist at Kom Abu Billo. The goddess's name, Aphrodite-Isis, reflects a blending of Greek and Egyptian religion.

beautiful statuette of a goddess, and I fell even more in love with archaeology.

At the end of each season of excavation at Kom Abu Billo, it was my job to take all of the artifacts we had found to the Cairo Museum, which was about 120 miles away. Many of the objects were of gold and all of them were very valuable, so I traveled in a truck that was guarded by soldiers.

In my first year, as soon as I had finished unloading the artifacts, I was told that there was a phone call for me. It was my cousin, telling me that my aunt had died. The second year, on the same day that I delivered the objects to the museum, I found out that one of my uncles had died!

The third year, I asked my boss to send someone else to the museum. He laughed at me, but only a few minutes later, a telegram arrived telling me that my beloved cousin Fayed had died in a bad accident. Reason, of course, told me that the deaths in my family were coincidences. Even so, that was the last year that I agreed to take the artifacts to the museum, and since I was put in charge of the excavations the next year, no one argued with me.

THE GOLDEN MUMMIES

Since 1996, I have been working in an oasis called Bahariya, which is 225 miles southwest of Cairo. We recently discovered there an enormous cemetery full of mummies. Many of the mummies are decorated with shining gold leaf, so I christened the site the "Valley of the Golden Mummies." In our first season of excavation (in 1999), we found five large tombs and a total of 105 mummies. One tomb, which we call Tomb 54, held 43 mummies covered with gold, including several children. Over the course of three seasons, we have found more than 250 mummies. They date to the later periods of Egyptian history, mostly to Roman times.

Many people wanted me to open the Valley of the Golden Mummies to tourists, but I refused to do this. Tourists are very dangerous to archaeological sites, and hordes of people trampling all over the ancient tombs would do them terrible damage. I also think it is important to respect the dead. Mummies are not objects for our amusement, they are the bodies of real people who wanted to live forever in the afterlife. Putting them on display feels wrong to me.

Dating to the days of Roman rule, this statue of the god Bes was found in a temple in the Bahariya Oasis. People of that time associated Bes with pleasure, wine, fertility, and childbirth.

The Valley of the Golden Mummies was discovered when the donkey of antiquities guard Abdul Maougoud stumbled into a hole that led to a tomb.

However, I eventually decided to sacrifice five of the mummies from Tomb 54 for the good of the rest of the site and its ghosts. By agreeing to move these five mummies from Tomb 54 to a new museum in the village nearby, I could be sure that the rest of the mummies would be safe, and that people could see what the mummies looked like

 MY REAL-LIFE BRUSHES WITH THE CURSE

without invading the delicate tombs. Two of the mummies I sent to the museum were children: a little boy of five and a younger girl. I decided, because of the way the mummies were decorated and where they were found in the tomb, that they were probably brother and sister. There was also a young man with them, and I believed he was their father.

HAUNTED DREAMS

I moved the mummies to the museum and finished the excavation season in July. After I got back to Cairo, I began to prepare myself to travel to the United States to teach archaeology at UCLA, where I spend every summer. I went to Los Angeles and settled in to start my course.

But the golden children had followed me to California, and they were haunting my dreams. I was having so much trouble sleeping that I could hardly wake up in the morning. The children, still wrapped in the white linen we had used to transport them to the museum, reached out their arms to me, trying to grab me. Another mummy we had put on display, a woman, also appeared in my dreams, looking at me with pleading eyes.

I had to do many TV and magazine interviews about the new discovery because the story of the golden mummies had been published on the front page of the *New York Times*. In mid-July, I was invited to give a lecture in Richmond, Virginia, at the Museum of Art. During the week before the talk, the children visited my dreams almost every night. In my worst nightmare, the little girl came for me.

A guard patrols this site in the Bahariya Oasis, where a multi-chambered tomb lies carved into the stone under the sand. Unlike earlier Egyptian mummies, very few of the golden mummies were buried in coffins.

She reached her slender white arms toward me and tried to wrap them around my throat. I could not understand why the children were disturbing my rest.

On the day of my talk, I was to fly to Richmond at 7 o'clock in the morning. I set my alarm clock for 4:30, but it didn't ring, so I didn't get up until 5 o'clock. I had to race to the airport without even washing my face, and I barely made my flight. I arrived in Philadelphia only to find that my connecting flight to Richmond had been canceled. I had to take a later flight to a city near Richmond and then take a taxi. I landed only an hour before my lecture, and the taxi driver got lost on the way, so I was late to the museum.

Everyone was waiting for me, but I asked the museum curator to show me to a bathroom so I could shave and change my clothes. I took off everything to wash, and then I discovered that there was no water! I had to get dressed again and find another bathroom. I finally gave my talk two hours late, and I found myself talking about the curse of the mummies, although I didn't mention my nightmares.

The next morning, I was supposed to give a talk to a school group at 9 o'clock. I had asked for a wake-up call, but

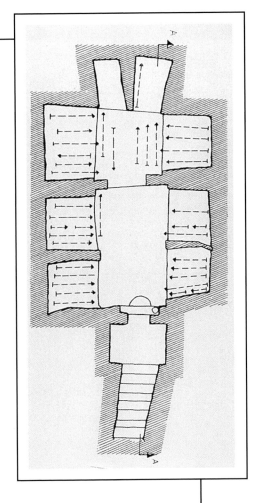

This sketch shows the layout of one of the ancient tombs in the Bahariya Oasis. Like many of the mummies found there, the one at left was adorned with a finely decorated layer of plaster painted with gold.

 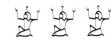

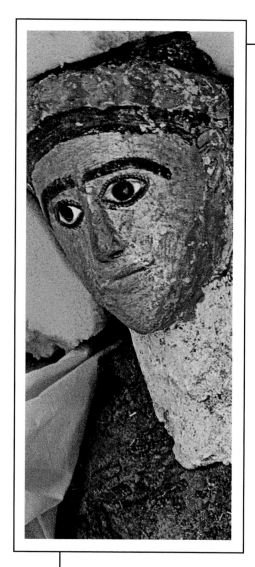

This is the boy mummy I had moved to a new resting place in a museum. His body is not quite three feet tall. We think that the boy was about five years old when he died.

I forgot and took the phone off the hook. I tossed and turned all night. The children came closer and closer, and frightened me in my sleep, until I finally awoke at 9:30 to hear my escort banging at my door. I did talk to the school group, but I'm not completely sure how much sense I made!

I realized that I could not ignore the golden children anymore. Later that morning, as I waited for my airplane back to Los Angeles, I forced myself to remember every detail of the children's faces. Suddenly I understood what they had been trying to tell me: They wanted their father to come with them to the museum. When I got back to Bahariya at the end of September 1999, I had the father moved to the museum so he could be with his son and daughter. The children never haunted me again.

THE GOVERNOR'S TOMB

I had another mysterious adventure in the Bahariya Oasis at a site called Sheikh Soby, which lies under the modern town of El Bawiti. In 1999, two young men told me that they could show me tombs hidden beneath some of the houses in the town. When I asked them what they

wanted in return, they told me that they just wanted jobs with the Antiquities Service. I am always suspicious of people who tell me about tombs, because I hate to waste my time on wild-goose chases. During my career, I have heard many stories from villagers about treasures of gold hidden under the ground. Several times in the past I have gone to investigate a spot and found absolutely nothing.

However, these young men seemed serious, so I decided to listen to what they had to say. They took me to the house of an old woman. There was a shaft under one of the rooms, and they tied me to a rope and let me down about 25 feet. To my amazement, I found myself inside a tomb decorated with scenes of ancient Egyptian gods and goddesses. I could not believe my eyes. I was sorry that I had not believed the boys at first, and I did give them jobs.

There turned out to be several tombs cut into the rock under this house and the ones surrounding it. These had been discovered 50 years ago by an archaeologist named Ahmed Fakhry. But then they had been lost to archaeologists, who were unable to pinpoint their exact location from Fakhry's descriptions, until the young men led us to them again. They had been lost

Thought to be the sister of the boy at left, this girl mummy seems to be smiling. In my dreams, these two children followed me wherever I turned—until I realized why they were troubled.

 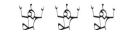

because local villagers had built houses on top of them, in direct violation of the law. By putting their houses on top of the tombs, they could explore them whenever they wanted and steal whatever treasures might have been left behind by robbers from ancient times.

The tombs belonged to a powerful family of the 26th Dynasty who had lived in the oasis between 664 and 525 B.C. The most important family members were also represented in the local temple, and we knew that one of them, Zed-khonsu-iuf-ank, had been governor of Bahariya. Fakhry had looked for, but never found, his tomb.

At the end of our first season of excavation in these lost tombs, we made a remarkable find. Through a crack in the wall of one of the original tombs, we caught a glimpse of a never-before-discovered tomb. I could see that it contained a huge sarcophagus, and I hoped that it would be the tomb of Zed-khonsu-iuf-ankh.

A CLOUD OF GOLDEN DUST

We had to wait until the beginning of the next season before we could explore this new tomb properly. On our return to Bahariya, our first priority was to open the tomb.

The tombs of an ancient governor and his family lie in a maze of chambers beneath local homes in the town of El Bawiti (left). Current residents were relocated so that we could excavate the tombs. Above, a worker's face shows just how dusty old tombs can be.

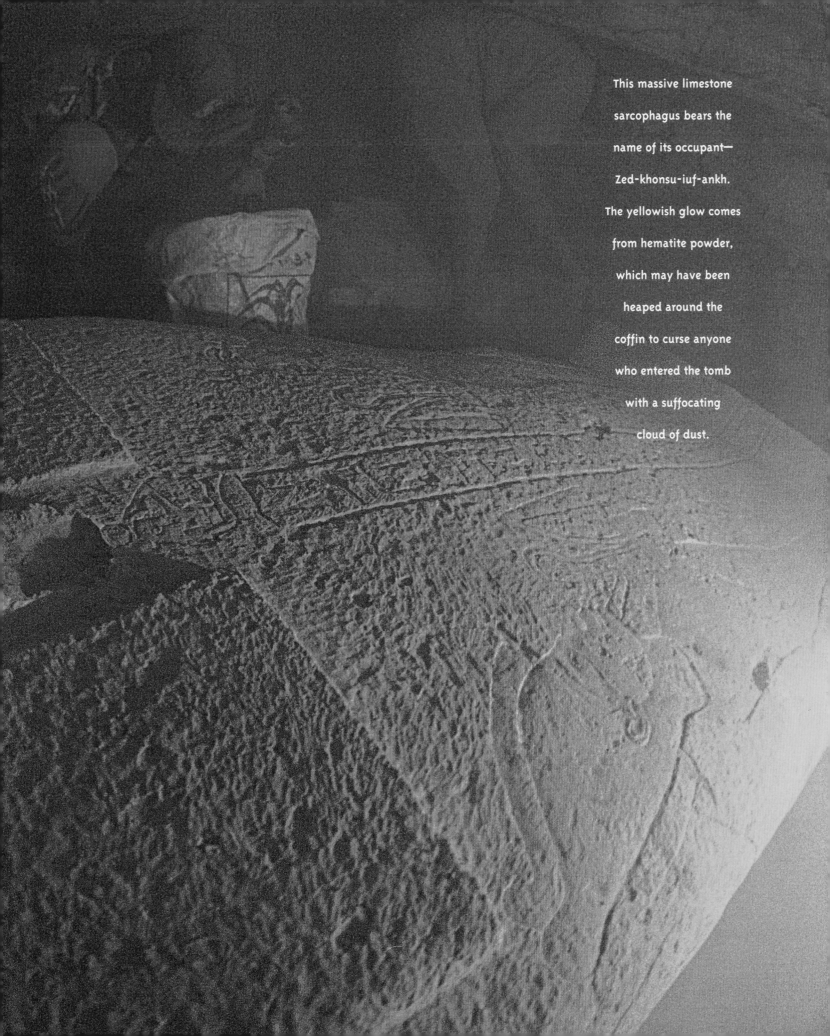

This massive limestone sarcophagus bears the name of its occupant—Zed-khonsu-iuf-ankh. The yellowish glow comes from hematite powder, which may have been heaped around the coffin to curse anyone who entered the tomb with a suffocating cloud of dust.

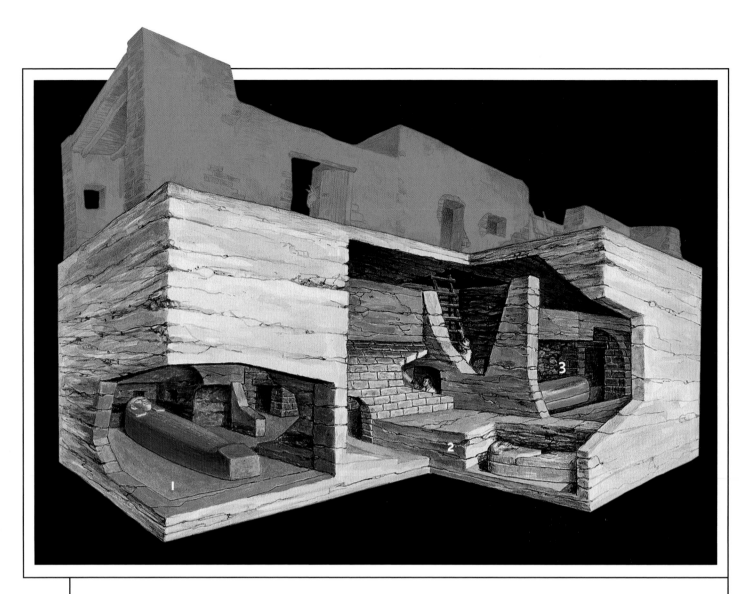

This diagram shows the location of the tombs of Zed-khonsu-iuf-ankh (1), his father (2), and his wife Naesa (3). In order to enter these tombs, we had to demolish the houses built over them.

We spent the first few days getting everything ready for the big event.

The night before we opened the tomb, I didn't speak with anyone at dinner, and I went to bed early to be alone with my thoughts. I had been thinking about this tomb for almost a year, and I could hardly wait for the next day. That night, I dreamed that I was inside a dark, smoke-filled room with no end and no way out. I called for help, but no one came. Then

MY REAL-LIFE BRUSHES WITH THE CURSE

a tall man came toward me, with the face I had seen on the sarcophagus through the crack in the wall. I tried to fight and tried to escape, but he kept coming toward me, and I could not get away. Finally I woke up. It was the middle of the night, and I was drenched with sweat.

The next morning, I stood before the entrance to the tomb, thinking about my nightmare. My architect, Abdel Hamied El-Kotb, came to tell me that the tomb was ready to

Workers use heavy ropes to remove the lid of the alabaster coffin that lay within the sarcophagus of Zed-khonsu-iuf-ankh. The wooden coffin and mummy inside it had decayed.

enter. The tomb had needed a great deal of preparation to make it safe, because sewage from the illegal houses above had been leaking down for years, eating away at the rock into which the tomb was carved. The walls were wet and crumbling, and there could have been a cave-in at any moment.

A friend who had come to watch took me aside and said, "You should let one of your assistants enter first. Aren't you afraid that the chamber could be full of snakes? Or something worse?"

I told him, "I would never do something like that! I am always the first to enter." I would never send one of my assistants into danger that I was afraid to face myself, and this habit has always brought me good luck. You cannot imagine the thrill of entering a place that has been hidden beneath the sands for thousands of years. I feel connected to my ancestors, as if I understand them better than anyone else.

And so that day I entered the tomb, trying not to think of my dream and my old fear of the dark. I took a flashlight with me and shone it toward the face of the sarcophagus. I was excited and happy—the moment of discovery is for me the breath of life, the moment that makes everything worthwhile. But as I walked toward the sarcophagus, I felt as though arrows of fire were attacking me. A cloud of yellow dust filled the room, and I could scarcely breathe because of the horrible smell. I considered going back until we could find out what the yellow powder surrounding me was, but the adventurer in me pushed on. I put my hand over my mouth and ran toward the sarcophagus, feeling as if I was dying. I held my nose so I could not smell, and I plunged on.

As I reached the sarcophagus, I could see that the face on it was beautifully modeled. On the sides were figures of Osiris, god of the dead, and lines of hieroglyphs.

I read through them very quickly and saw right away that the name included the "Zed" sign. I had found the tomb of the governor, Zed-khonsu-iuf-ankh. It took us six days and more than 60 plastic bags to clear the powder from the tomb. It turned out to be hematite, a mineral that was ground and used for paint. I do not know whether the powder was left over from the painting of the tomb or whether it was heaped around the sarcophagus to curse anyone who entered the tomb.

When the powder was cleared, we could investigate the sarcophagus. The lid weighed about 12 tons, so I asked my architect to call brothers Talal and Ahmed El-Krity, experts in moving heavy stones. They had been trained by their father, who had been trained by his father, and so on back into the mists of time. Their ancestors had moved heavy stones, perhaps even for the pharaohs themselves.

Talal and Ahmed came, and we worked together in the burial chamber. We set a date to open the lid of the sarcophagus and got ready. But then a call came telling the brothers that their father had died, and they had to go home. All the people in the village of Sheikh Soby thought that this was the "Curse of the Governor." But several days later, the men came back, and we opened the lid successfully.

A SHOCKING EXPERIENCE

My adventures in the Bahariya Oasis were not over. A break in the shaft leading to the tomb of the governor brought us to a room full of sand. In the north wall of this room was the entrance to a second chamber, closed with sandstone blocks. I began to excavate this with a lamp in my left hand and an ax in my right hand. After about

a foot, I glimpsed the head of an alabaster sarcophagus, so I pushed the lamp forward to see better. The wire to the lamp snapped, and I got an electric shock that knocked me unconscious. After a few minutes, I opened my eyes and saw all of my assistants looking down at me. One asked me, "What happened? Are you all right?" I jumped up and said that I was OK. I asked them if they realized that if I had died, this would be the main headline in all the newspapers: "The Curse of the Pharaohs Strikes Again!" I could not believe that I was safe, although I could feel the electricity still shaking my body for the next few hours.

This tomb turned out to belong to Naesa, wife of the governor Zed-khonsu-iuf-ankh. It had been robbed long ago, but the thieves had not stolen everything—we found 239 ushabti and 103 pieces of gold. Naesa's mummy had been badly damaged by the robbers, but we could tell that she had been very short, only about four and a half feet tall, and that she had lived into old age. Some might say that the shock I received was proof of the mummy's evil curse. But I look at it another way. I feel that instead of trying to harm me, Naesa must have been looking after me, protecting me so that the electricity did not kill me.

In the tomb of Naesa we found 239 ushabti. These small figures of servants or farm workers were placed in a tomb in the belief that they would perform chores for the deceased in the afterlife.

Dangers and Rewards

NAESA'S SARCOPHAGUS, LIKE HER HUSBAND'S, was surrounded by hematite powder. Even though it was February, it was very warm, which makes it easier for germs to grow. The dust got into my ears, and I got an infection, although I did not know it at the time. I went back to Cairo for my son Karim's graduation from college, and while I was there, I went to a party arranged by the American University Press in Cairo for their authors. Mark Linz, the head of the press, asked me to give a speech. While Mark was introducing me, I suddenly felt as though the ceiling and the floor had traded places. I became very dizzy, and grabbed the hand of a friend, an Egyptologist named

Archaeology can be dangerous, backbreaking work. Here a worker shovels rubble from a tomb. The walls are supported by beams to keep them from caving in.

Salima Ikram, who was sitting next to me. She tried to help me, but she couldn't hold me up. I fell, and couldn't get up. I could hear everyone around me talking, but couldn't answer. I was afraid I would die!

Mark and his assistant, Nabila, called an ambulance. By the time it arrived I had recovered a little and managed to get back on my chair. The ambulance took me to the emergency room, but no one could find out what was wrong with me. I went home, but I continued to feel dizzy. Finally, a doctor suggested that I might have an ear infection and put me on antibiotics. A week later, I was completely better, but rumors flew that I had had a heart attack and was dying.

FACING FIRE AND CATCHING THIEVES

My life as an archaeologist has always been exciting and full of danger, from the very beginning. I thought that my first assignment in the antiquities department, as an Inspector at Tuna el-Gebel, would be boring. But soon after I arrived, as I told you earlier, I began to love it, and I had many adventures there.

While I was at Tuna el-Gebel, there was a fire that burned for more than three weeks in some underground galleries where mummified birds and baboons were buried. These animals were sacred to the god Thoth, the god of wisdom. We fought the fire for ten days, but as soon as the fire department stopped pumping water, the galleries began to burn again. We finally brought in an expert, an architect named Mamdouh Yacoub, who had us build a wall at the entrance to the galleries so that the air supply to the fire would be cut off. The fire did burn itself out, but it took two weeks.

I had my first brush with tomb robbers at Tuna el-Gebel. The police chief for the nearest town came to me one day to tell me that he had a tip about a family that was doing some antiquities smuggling. He picked me up the next day at dawn, and we went to pay a surprise visit to a house in the village nearby. We arrived, and the police knocked at the door. The man inside refused to open the door, so we broke it down. Inside, in the courtyard of the house, the man and his family were digging up antiquities—broken statues and pottery—to sell on the black market. The man yelled at me, "Why are you here? These things belong to me, they belonged to my ancestors, and you have no right to take them!" But he was breaking the law, so the police took him to jail.

Several years later, in 1973, I was working as an inspector at Abu Simbel, which is in the far south of Egypt. There are two beautiful temples there, cut into the rocks of the Nubian cliffs. Both of these temples were built during the New Kingdom by Ramses II, also known as Ramses the Great. While I was there, there was a big robbery at Giza. There was a rest house there, to the south of the pyramids, which had been built for President Nassar. He didn't like staying there, so the antiquities service used it to store artifacts. Hundreds of objects were there, collected from excavations all over the region.

One evening, a group of thieves from the village at the foot of the pyramids broke a hole in the northern wall of this building and stole some of the boxes of artifacts. This was a great scandal. How could they have done this? Where were the guards? Where were the police? And where were the artifacts?

I had already become known as a strong man who could get things done.

Carved into rock, this temple at Abu Simbel honors Ramses II. The four gigantic seated figures portray the pharaoh. The smaller, standing figures represent his family members.

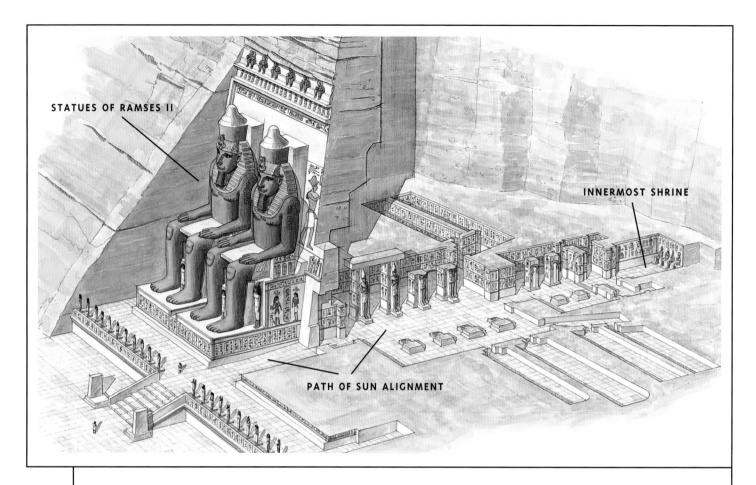

STATUES OF RAMSES II

INNERMOST SHRINE

PATH OF SUN ALIGNMENT

As seen in this cutaway diagram, the temple of Ramses II at Abu Simbel extended deep inside the rocky cliffs. Twice each year, rays of the setting sun penetrated to shine on statues of the gods in the innermost part of the shrine.

The head of the Antiquities Service called me right away and asked me to leave Abu Simbel and come to Giza to take charge. I came the next day, and I spent the next month looking for the stolen antiquities. My colleague Ahmed el-Sawy and I went with the police from house to house searching for the stolen objects. The thieves soon became frightened, and they dumped the artifacts in the Mansouria canal, which lies near the foot of the plateau.

After the objects were recovered, I turned my attention to creating stability at Giza so that such a theft could never

DANGERS AND REWARDS

happen again. One way I did this was to pay surprise visits to the plateau in the middle of the night to make sure the guards were at their posts.

MYSTERIOUS MAGIC

At Tuna el-Gebel, I also experienced for the first time the mysterious magic of ancient Egypt. One day, I was sitting in my office when a well-dressed man and woman came to visit the site. The man was a doctor, and the woman had a degree in business. I invited them to drink tea, and they told me that they had been married for eight years but had not been able to have a child. Although none of the many doctors they had gone to see in Cairo and Alexandria had been able to help them, they had not lost hope. They had come to Tuna el-Gebel because some people in their village had told them about a magic place inside the temple of Thoth, god of wisdom, where there was a monument to Min, the god of fertility. The couple had been told that if the wife stood above a specific stone, she would get pregnant.

I laughed and said, "How can a man with your education believe in something like this?" He answered that

Thoth, the god of wisdom, was sometimes portrayed as a baboon (above) and sometimes as an ibis or as an ibis-headed man. This god was also associated with writing and magic.

DANGERS AND REWARDS

99

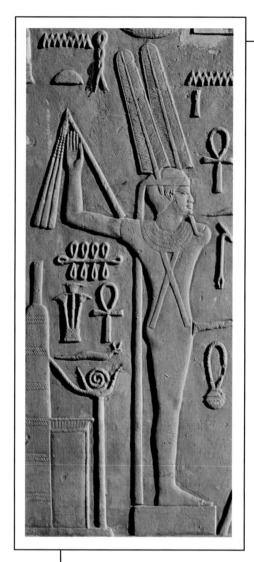

he did believe it was true and asked if I could show them the spot.

I thought it was ridiculous, but I asked the chief of the guards to take them to the temple of Thoth and Min. Then I forgot about them. But a year later, they came to visit me and brought their three-month-old son, whom they had dedicated to Min. I could not believe my eyes.

Perhaps this sort of unexplainable wonder has helped me in my determination to face any danger in order to protect our past. Since the beginning of my career, I have been resolved to stop antiquities thieves from robbing us of our heritage.

HAZARDOUS WORK

This carving depicts Min, the god of fertility. To my amazement and wonder, nine months after a childless couple visited Min's temple at Tuna el-Gebel, the wife gave birth to a son.

I will tell you about one more adventure. This happened to me at the site of Abydos, which is in the remote desert of Middle Egypt. This is the site where the first kings of Egypt were buried, and where the god Osiris was worshipped throughout Egyptian history.

There is an excavation house at the site, and at the time it had only a small outdoor bathroom, built of mud brick with a wooden door and no roof. One night I was inside

this bathroom when I heard a knocking on the door. I said that I would be right out, but the knocking continued. I called out again, but it did not stop. Finally I got nervous and climbed up on the wooden seat to look over the top of the wall. Outside was a huge cobra, knocking its head against the door! I am very glad that I did not let it in.

Such adventures, and many others, make up the story of my life as an archaeologist. I have been very lucky, and I have either survived or avoided many disasters. I imagine that there are those who would attribute everything bad that happens to me to the curse of the pharaohs. But there are natural explanations for most of the accidents that are chalked up to the curse.

Whether or not we believe in ancient magic and curses, however, there is no doubt that archaeology can be hazardous. As explorers, we routinely enter dark tunnels without knowing what we will find, and we open chambers that have been sealed for thousands of years. We are often in danger from crumbling rock, sudden drops, poisonous insects and snakes, from modern tomb robbers, and from ancient germs.

ANCIENT GERMS

Imagine that we mummify several bodies by dehydrating them, removing their internal organs, and wrapping them carefully in linen. The mummies are then put in a small room with some food and drink and maybe some flowers, and the room is locked and made airtight.

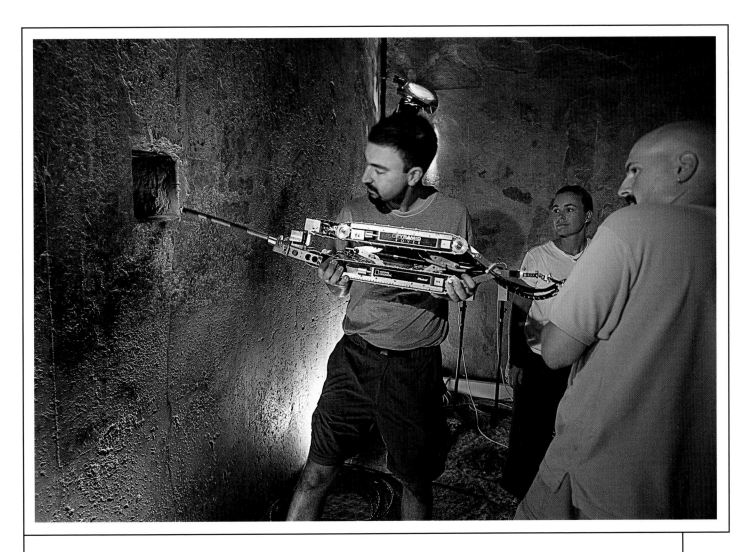

When the room is opened again 3,000 years later, it seems impossible that anything at all could still be living in there. Yet the room will very likely contain ancient germs, which we cannot see but which have nonetheless survived for all that time. Indeed, some archaeologists have gotten sick—and some have even died—because they entered sealed chambers without taking the proper precautions.

To avoid germs, a worker wears a mask while cleaning a mummy (left). Not all archaeological exploration is done by humans. Above, a robotic probe is sent to investigate a shaft.

DANGERS AND REWARDS

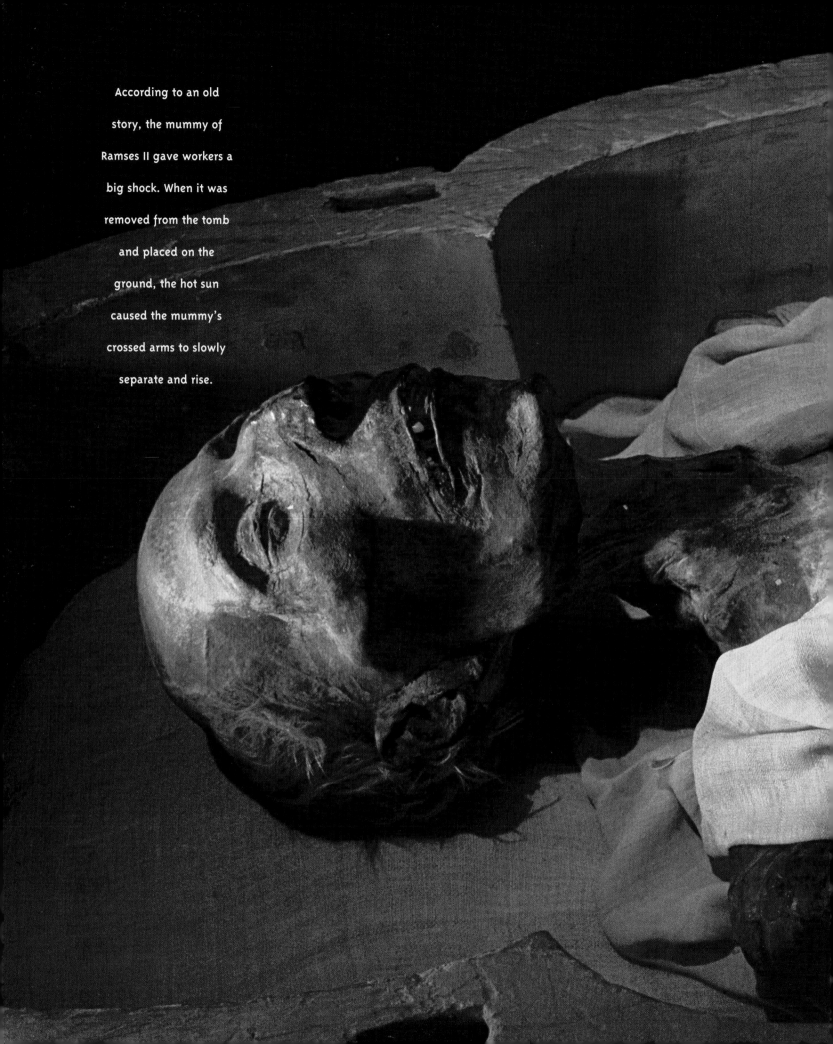

According to an old story, the mummy of Ramses II gave workers a big shock. When it was removed from the tomb and placed on the ground, the hot sun caused the mummy's crossed arms to slowly separate and rise.

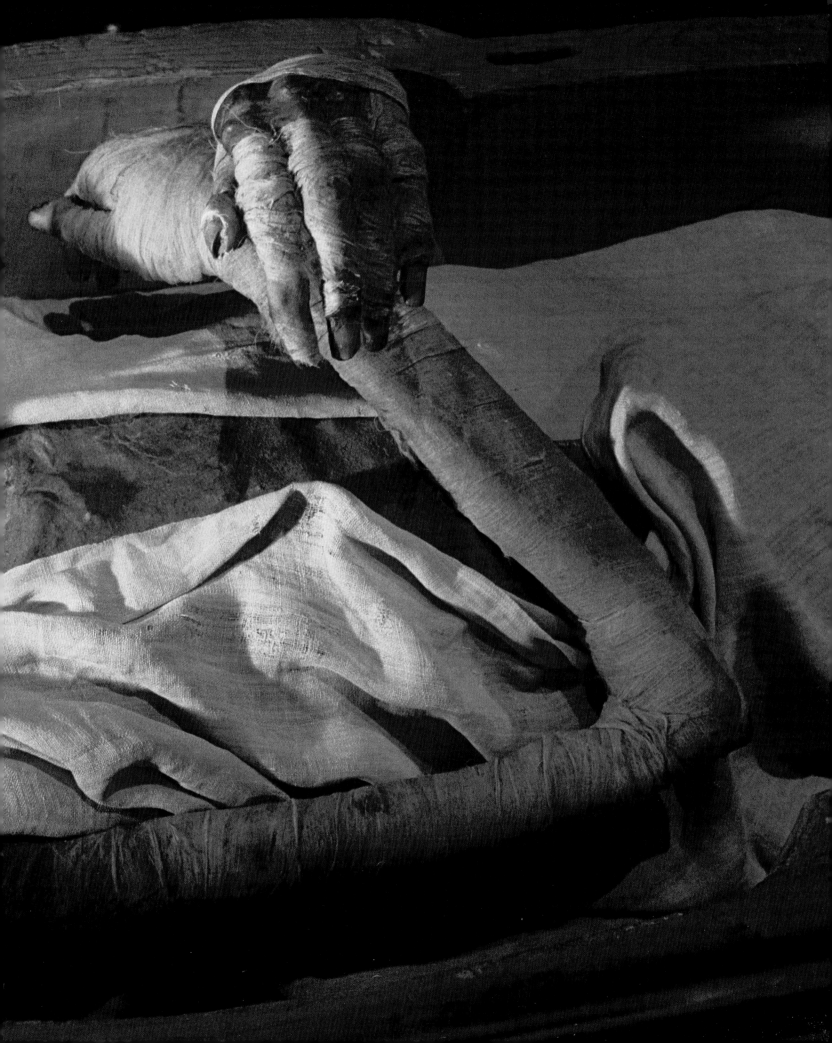

A symbol of royal power, Horus, the falcon god of kings, embraces King Khafre in this statue. Builder of the second pyramid at Giza, Khafre was the son of King Khufu.

When I find an intact burial chamber, I open it, but I do not allow anyone to enter right away. I leave it open for two days so that the foul air can escape. And then I go in first. I never shave on the days when I am entering a new tomb, since shaving opens the pores and allows germs to enter and cause infection. I advise my assistants to wear masks when they work on the mummies that we find (which, by the way, smell awful).

I am currently arranging a new project with the Institute of Nuclear Research to scientifically study the germs that lurk inside ancient tombs. I am hoping that we will find out exactly what sort of bacteria can survive the millennia. This will give us more information about the past and help to protect us for the future.

GREAT DISCOVERIES

Despite the dangers that are involved in exploring the past, I treasure every moment, because the rewards are so great. Imagine finding a statue that has been buried in the sand for 3,000 years, brushing off the sand, and looking into its

beautiful eyes. These are the moments I live for. Making connections with our ancient past is my passion in life. It makes all the dangers worthwhile. I have been fortunate to make many wonderful discoveries, following in the footsteps of the great archaeologists of the past.

The past century and a half has been a rich and important one for Egyptology. Many exciting discoveries have been made during this time, some as or more exciting than the tomb of Tutankhamun. There are so many of these that I could write another book. But for now, I will tell you about a few of my favorites.

One of the most beautiful royal statues is one of King Khafre, who was the builder of the Second Pyramid at Giza. This statue was found inside a hole dug in the entrance hall of his valley temple, where 23 statues once stood. I believe that this masterpiece, along with fragments of other statues, was hidden inside the hole by priests who lived during the First Intermediate Period. This was a time of chaos in Egypt, when the royal line of the Old Kingdom had lost control of the country. The pyramids were robbed then and the temples smashed. But some loyal priests tried to protect what was left, and they put this statue in a deep hole to protect it from the vandals.

In the statue, Khafre seems to breathe, and the artist has made the royal blood seem to flow beneath the hard stone of his skin. Behind him, embracing his head, is a falcon. If you look at the statue from the side, you will feel that the falcon is flying with the king to the sky. This statue also represents the divine triad of Osiris, god of the dead (the king), his wife Isis (the throne, which is the hieroglyph for the name of Isis), and their son Horus (the falcon). The stone from which the statue

 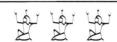

is carved came from Nubia, 600 miles to the south. The name of Khafre has been found carved in quarries there.

Another exciting discovery was the royal tombs at Tanis. In 1939, French archaeologists excavating in the north of Egypt found the rich, unrobbed tombs of the kings who ruled the land in about 1000 B.C. This was near the end of the pharaonic period, when Egypt was already in decline. The beautiful coffins in which the royal bodies were laid to rest gleam with the warm glow of gold and shimmer with the cold light of silver. These extraordinary treasures give us an idea of the wealth that even these later kings commanded.

I have already told you about one of the greatest discoveries in Egyptian archaeology, the cache of royal mummies found near the Valley of the Kings by the Abd el-Rassul family. The cache included Ramses the Great and his father, Seti I, along with ten other monarchs. As I mentioned before, the authorities found out about the discovery in 1881 and took the mummies to Cairo for safe-keeping. As the boat in which the bodies rested floated down the Nile, the people of Egypt lined the banks to give their ancient kings a royal farewell.

The coffin of Ramses I (the grandfather of Ramses the Great) was in this cache, but the king's mummy was missing. Several years ago, an Egyptologist discovered a royal mummy in a small collection in a museum at Niagara Falls, New York. The style of mummification and the position of the arms identified it as a king of the late 18th or early 19th dynasty (the period just after the death of Tutankhamun).

In 1996, the Michael C. Carlos Museum in Atlanta, Georgia, obtained this mummy and the other Egyptian objects in the Niagara Falls collection.

Ancient Egypt holds endless fascination. Here, tourists at an Egyptian museum enjoy a statue of Ramses the Great.

Egyptologists at the museum spent several years studying this mummy and concluded that it is most likely Ramses I. In October 2003, I traveled to Atlanta and came home with this royal mummy, a gift from the Michael C. Carlos Museum and the people of Atlanta to the people of Egypt. We brought him, wrapped in linen and packed carefully in a wooden box, to the Cairo Museum. A ceremony was held the next day at which Egyptian children dressed like the ancient pharaohs sang to welcome this great king home.

These discoveries, along with many others, tell us stories of an ancient people, and of how ordinary and extraordinary men and women built a civilization that has captured our hearts. I believe that the ancient Egyptians would never curse us. They would want their stories told so that their names are not lost forever in the sands of time.

DANGERS AND REWARDS

The Truth About the Curse

SO, IS THERE AN ANCIENT CURSE THAT HAUNTS those who disturb the dead? Although it is true that Carter's canary was eaten by a cobra, I can tell you that all the rest of the curse stories about the tomb of Tutankhamun and the other tragedies attributed to the curse were either made up completely or have simple, natural explanations:

> This statue of the jackal-headed god Anubis, protector of the dead, guarded the entrance to the treasury in Tutankhamun's tomb.

* Lord Carnarvon himself had a weak constitution—he had originally come to Egypt to improve his health, permanently damaged in 1901 when his newfangled automobile went out of control at the alarming speed of 20 miles per hour. So it is not so strange that he would die from an infection and

pneumonia. After all, at the time there were no antibiotics available to treat these conditions.

* The lights in Cairo may well have gone off when Carnarvon died—the electricity in Cairo was totally unreliable in the 1920s, and the lights went off and on all the time.

* Lord Carnarvon died at 4 o'clock in the morning, Egyptian time, which would have been about 2 o'clock English time. His son was in India at the time, so it seems very odd that he could have known firsthand, as he claimed, of the exact time of death of his father's favorite dog.

* The mosquito bite on Carnarvon's cheek was actually not in the same place as a scar on Tutankhamun's face.

* The golden canopic shrine, said to have an ominous curse inscription, bears only standard religious spells.

* The mud brick found near the statue of Anubis, said to bear a curse, actually reads: "I am the one who prevents the sand from blocking the secret chamber."

EXPLAINING THE DEATHS

All of the deaths said to be caused by the curse actually had logical explanations:

* The workman who first saw the statues of Rahotep and Nofret at Meidum and had an immediate heart attack was most likely overcome not by fear but by unbearable excitement, since he would have known that the reward

for this extraordinary find would most likely feed his family for many years.

* Mohammed Mahdy, head of the Egyptian Antiquities Organization in 1977, was killed crossing Tahrir Square, the busiest place in Cairo. This is a huge traffic circle with cars coming very fast from about eight different directions and no one paying any attention to pedestrians.

* Dr. Mehrez, the other head of the Egyptian Antiquities Organization who died while in office, was an Islamic archaeologist, and he had never touched a tomb from the pharaonic period! In addition, he had been ailing for a long time and was considered at risk of having a heart attack at any time.

One of my professors at the University of Pennsylvania, David Silverman, was asked to testify as an expert witness at the trial of the man who claimed that an ancient statuette he had brought home from Egypt had commanded him to kill his wife. Dr. Silverman found that the ushabti was a fake. (The man was found guilty.)

Those believing in Tutankhamun's curse should surely have expected that the people most closely associated with the excavation would be in the most danger. But Howard Carter himself lived for more than 17 years after the discovery, dying at the age of 64 in his home in England. Lord Carnarvon's daughter, who was one of the first people to enter the tomb, lived for another 58 years, dying at age 79.

About a decade after the discovery of Tut's tomb, American Egyptologist Herbert Winlock did his own statistical study of the curse. He found that as of 1934, out of the 26 people present at the opening of the tomb, only six had died; out of the 22 people present at the opening of the sarcophagus, only two had died.

Howard Carter brushes
off King Tut's inner
coffin. Despite his close
involvement with Tut's
excavation, Carter seems
to have escaped any
curse. He lived for
another 17 years.

All of the ten people present at the unwrapping of the mummy (clearly the most dangerous moment of all) were still alive.

AN ONGOING THREAT

The dearest wish of the ancient Egyptian was to have his or her name live forever. Tutankhamun, after languishing in complete obscurity for thousands of years, would likely be grateful rather than angry that his tomb was discovered. He is now the best known and most talked about of all Egyptian kings, and his name is spoken with a frequency that he could never have imagined. So I don't believe he would place a curse on those who found him.

If there really were a curse, antiquities thieves should suffer from it the most. But the reality is that very few ancient tombs have been found intact, and most tomb robbers seem to have escaped without harm. Of course, there were exceptions: In one tomb from a site called Riqqa, excavators found the skeleton of a tomb robber who had been crushed by falling debris just as he was lifting the mummy out of its coffin. I have already told you the story of Paser and Pawera, and there were other robbers who were also caught and punished by the authorities. But on the whole, it appears that antiquities thieves have survived and prospered. Robbing tombs has been a lucrative profession for thousands of years, and it is still practiced today. If there is a curse of the pharaohs, it doesn't seem to be very effective. I have dedicated myself to fighting modern antiquities thieves, but I have to admit that I am not counting on the curse to help me.

The wonderful works our ancestors left in the sands of Egypt are in danger, threatened by modern tomb robbers and antiquities dealers, by unthinking tourists, by the rising water table, and by the exploding population of Egypt. If we do not rescue them, the information we could gain from them and the beauty we could enjoy will be lost to us forever. Through the science of archaeology, we can enter the world of the ancient Egyptians. It is a world full of secrets and magic, where we can experience the glory of the ancient past.

When the tomb of Seti I was discovered in 1817, his mummy was missing. It was later found, inside this wooden coffin, in the secret cache of mummies discovered by the ancestors of my friend Sheikh Aly.

A NEW MYSTERY

The sands and cliffs of Egypt still hold many mysteries. I will tell you the story of one more secret. The tomb of Ramses I's son, Seti I, lies in the Valley of the Kings. It is the largest and most spectacular tomb in the valley. This tomb is perched high in the cliffs, and it is not easy to

 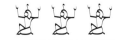

TO TOMB ENTRANCE

This illustration shows how the tomb of Seti I, in the Valley of the Kings, was built and decorated. Workers chipped away at the solid limestone cliffs to create steps, corridors, and rooms, which were then decorated.

enter. But when you finally reach the entrance corridor, you forget all the climbing and bending. The walls are covered with breathtakingly beautiful reliefs, some of the most exquisite you will ever see.

In 1973, when I first met Sheikh Aly, he predicted that one day I would be head of the Antiquities Service in Egypt. He also told me that another room lay at the end of a long tunnel that leads west from the burial chamber. After I became head of Egypt's antiquities, I began to think

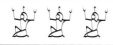 **THE TRUTH ABOUT THE CURSE**

again about the Sheikh's second prophesy. Most scholars would never pay attention to this type of information, but I have always followed my instincts. After all, Sheikh Aly's ancestors are probably the men who carved and painted the royal tombs (and possibly those who robbed them), and their memories are long. Without this family, the royal cache of mummies might never have been found.

On a recent visit to the Valley of the Kings, I decided to investigate Sheikh Aly's tunnel. With me were Terry

Paintings and sacred writings meant to guide and protect the dead king in his journey to the afterlife cover the inside of Seti I's tomb. Could there be another, yet-to-be-discovered chamber in the tomb?

Here, my friends Lisa Truitt and Terry Garcia and I are investigating an unexplored tunnel in Seti I's tomb. For safety's sake, we had to turn back—but I will return to see where it leads.

Garcia, vice president of the National Geographic Society, and Lisa Truitt, a National Geographic TV producer. Armed with only a flashlight, we descended into this tunnel. It was very dangerous—I kept banging my head, and rocks fell on us as we squeezed through the narrow space. We got only partway through before I decided it was too unsafe to continue, so we turned around. But I will return, and we will explore this tunnel scientifically. We will use

 THE TRUTH ABOUT THE CURSE

the most modern technology to shore up the walls and ceilings and make it safe to enter. Who knows what we will find?

BLESSED BY MY WORK

In my 30 years of excavating, I have never had an experience that I would attribute to an ancient curse. Instead, I have felt blessed by my work, and I have felt the gratitude of the ancient monuments that I have spent my life uncovering and preserving for the generations yet to come. And yet, as I've told you in this book, some strange things have happened to me that have made me wonder whether some sort of ancient Egyptian magic might be at work.

When I was young, I wanted to be a lawyer. But then I went to college and read some law books, and found that the law did not reach my heart. So I changed my mind. I had never dreamed of being an archaeologist, and I didn't even know exactly what one did. Even after studying at the university for four years, I was not convinced that I wanted to spend my life digging in the sand. I thought it would be much more glamorous to be a lawyer or a scientist, like people I saw in the movies. But on my first excavation, I discovered the beautiful statue I told you about earlier, and I found that what I really loved was archaeology. I have given my passion to my work, and I have made it into the most exciting and rewarding job in the world—exploring the past, searching for the unknown, reconstructing history. Every day for me is an adventure.

But I never worry about the curse.

A F T E R W O R D

ABOUT A YEAR AGO, I had a very special visitor. Her name is Dina, and she is about eight years old. She is an Egyptian-American. Before she came to Cairo she asked her aunt, "Do you know Zahi Hawass? I see him on TV, and it would be a dream to meet him while I am in Egypt." Her aunt replied that yes, she knew me, and that she would arrange for Dina to visit me.

Dina came to see me at my office in the shadow of the pyramids. She was so excited that she couldn't stand still, filled with anticipation and something I was surprised to see—fear! The first thing she said to me was, "I do not want to enter the Great Pyramid because of the curse." I tried to explain to her that there is no such thing as the curse and that the things she had heard were not true. I told her most of the stories from this book in the hope of reassuring her that she would be safe. But the more I spoke, the more unconvinced she was.

Finally, I told her that I would enter the Great Pyramid with her and that I would always be with her. We walked across the Giza plateau toward the pyramid. Dina's pace slowed with every step we took. She held my hand tightly. When we reached the Pyramid, the lights inside were off, and I told Dina that we would have an adventure in the dark. As we entered the Pyramid, the color drained from her face and she held my hand even tighter. In her free hand, she held a flashlight with which she lighted our way.

Dina looked at me with a mixture of trust, excitement, and terror. I began to explain the Pyramid to her. We were making our way through the dark passageways, bent double, inching forward, until we reached the second chamber, the Queen's chamber. By this time, Dina had relaxed a little, listening to my stories and feeling the magic and mystery of the Great Pyramid. In the Queen's chamber, I showed

This ivory figure of King Khufu, builder of the Great Pyramid, is only about two and a half inches tall. It is the only known statue of the powerful monarch.

I enjoyed introducing my young friend Dina to the Great Sphinx and the pyramids at Giza. After we explored the Great Pyramid together, she learned for herself the truth about the curse.

her the location of the narrow tunnels called airshafts that lead to secret doors. I told Dina that a team from National Geographic would send a robot into the airshafts soon to see what is behind these secret doors.

We continued our adventure as we left the second chamber and entered the Grand Gallery, the beautiful passageway leading to Khufu's burial chamber. By this time, Dina was more excited than afraid, and I could see her confidence grow with every step. We climbed and climbed up the dark passage until we reached the burial chamber. And then an amazing thing happened: She let go of my hand. In her excitement, she forgot her fear. She walked over to

AFTERWORD

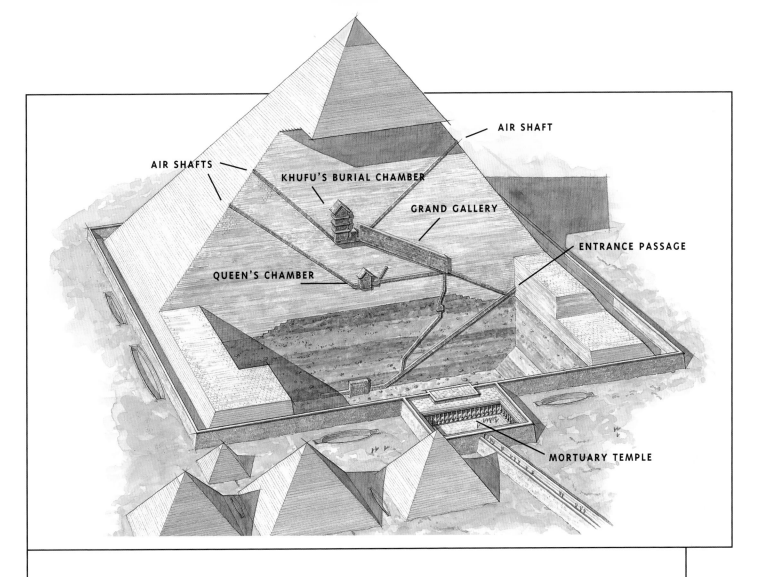

AIR SHAFT

AIR SHAFTS

KHUFU'S BURIAL CHAMBER

GRAND GALLERY

ENTRANCE PASSAGE

QUEEN'S CHAMBER

MORTUARY TEMPLE

Khufu's sarcophagus and told me with a bright smile on her face that she wanted to take a photo to show her friends at school.

We finished the visit and started to leave the Pyramid. Dina was walking on her own, no longer holding my hand. She had a happy bounce in her step. I could see with the light of the flashlight that she was not scared and that she was smiling from ear to ear. We quickly made our way through the dark passageways that had scared her before and now seemed to energize her, until we left the Pyramid and could feel the bright sun hit our faces. She blinked a few times to adjust to the bright light and then with a beautiful smile said to her aunt Lamia, "I do not believe in the curse!"

This diagram shows the approximate location of the airshafts that I pointed out to Dina when she and I explored the Great Pyramid together. I can't wait to see what the robots will find when they explore the shafts.

AFTERWORD

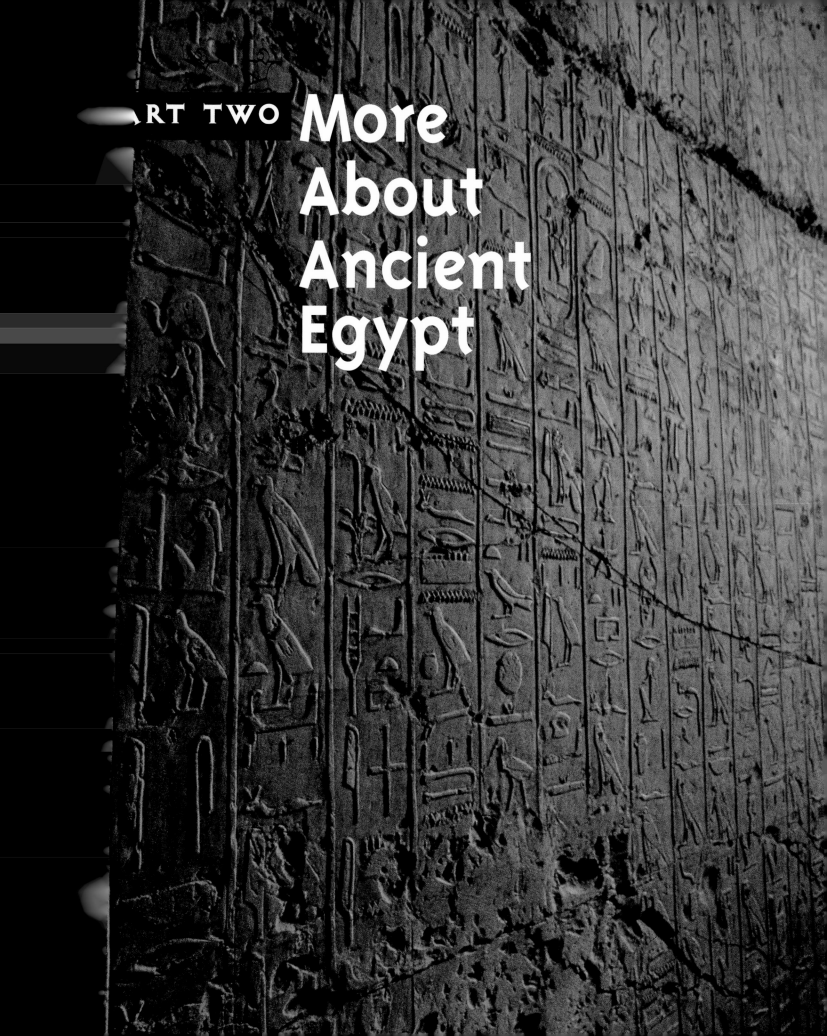

PART TWO

More About Ancient Egypt

Hieroglyphs carved into the entrance of Ramses II's tomb in Thebes praise this powerful pharaoh, who ruled over Egypt for 66 years. Every time I enter an ancient tomb, I feel more strongly connected to my ancestors and want to learn even more about them.

TIPS FOR
BECOMING AN ARCHAEOLOGIST

Young people often ask me how they, too, can became an archaeologist. Here is my advice:

* Read every book and magazine you can find on archaeology and ancient Egypt. The more you read, the more you will know, and the more fun you will have.

* Watch National Geographic television specials about archaeology and ancient Egypt. Then you can follow my adventures and experience the magic of archaeology through my eyes.

* Check out my Web site at guardians.net/hawass. I keep it updated, so you will always know the latest news.

* Study hard at school, and learn foreign languages such as French, German, and Arabic. You will need these languages to read important books and articles. Arabic is especially important. Not enough foreign archaeologists speak it now, so you will have a big head start if you do.

* Go to a college that teaches archaeology and Egyptology. Make sure you have good teachers, and learn how to write well.

* Go to a field school and learn to excavate. Then go on as many digs as you can. Nothing can replace the excitement of finding ancient artifacts. I encourage you to experience this thrill for yourself.

* Come to visit Egypt, and see all the archaeological sites you can.

* Have passion and love for the past.

* Be adventurous!

Archaeologists need to have a delicate touch. Here, I am carefully clearing sand from a mummy using a brush and a small handheld blower.

TRACING EGYPT'S GLORIOUS PAST:
A CHRONOLOGY

NEOLITHIC PERIOD
4500–3000 B.C.
* Agriculture is developed by this time.
* People are settled in villages.
* Rulers are local.
* Egypt is made up of two regions: Lower Egypt, centered in the Nile Delta, and Upper Egypt, along the river's path.

EARLY DYNASTIC PERIOD
3000–2650 B.C.
Dynasties 1—2
* Upper and Lower Egypt are united under one ruler, giving rise to the First Dynasty.
* Capital is built at Memphis.
* Egyptian scribes begin using hieroglyphs.
* Royal tombs are built at Abydos and Saqqara.

OLD KINGDOM
2650–2150 B.C.
Dynasties 3—6
* There is a strong centralized government and powerful rulers.
* Trade and arts flourish.

* Step Pyramid of Djoser is built at Saqqara.
* Great Pyramid of Khufu and other pyramids are built at Giza.
* Sphinx is carved at Giza to honor Khafre.
* Kings are worshiped as gods.
* Kings' power declines toward the end of this period.

FIRST INTERMEDIATE PERIOD
2150–2040 B.C.
Dynasties 7—11
* Drought, famine and disease may have contributed to disorder.
* Central government collapses.
* Egypt is divided into separate kingdoms led by local rulers.
* Separate kingdoms are often at war.

MIDDLE KINGDOM
2040–1640 B.C.
Dynasties 11—13
* Mentuhotep II, fifth king of Dynasty 11, reunites ancient Egypt.
* Peace and prosperity return.

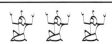

* Thebes becomes an important town.
* Capital is a little south of Memphis, at Itj-Tawy.
* Rulers are strong and powerful.
* Egypt conquers parts of Nubia (now called Sudan).
* Kings are buried in pyramids.

SECOND INTERMEDIATE PERIOD
1640–1550 B.C.

Dynasties 14–17
* Egypt again falls into disorder.
* Foreigners known as the Hyksos, probably from western Asia, take over the delta region of Egypt.
* The Hyksos rule the delta region for decades.

NEW KINGDOM
1550–1070 B.C.

Dynasties 18–20
* Ahmose I of Thebes drives the Hyksos out of Egypt.
* New territories are conquered and a great empire built.
* Egyptians enjoy great prosperity.
* Capitals are at Thebes amd Memphis.
* Rulers include Hatshepsut (a woman), Akhenaten, and Tutankhamun.
* Ramses II rules for 67 years, builds great temple at Abu Simbel.
* Burials are in the Valley of the Kings.
* Royal tombs are filled with gold, other riches.

THIRD INTERMEDIATE PERIOD
1070–712 B.C.

Dynasties 21–25
* Widespread government corruption contributes to collapse of New Kingdom.
* Egypt is divided into separate kingdoms.
* Kings from Nubia (Sudan) and Libya rule during some of this period.

LATE PERIOD
712–332 B.C.

Dynasties 26–31
* Assyrians from Asia invade Egypt and destroy its great cities.
* Persians conquer Egypt.
* Last native Egyptian rulers are in power.

GRECO-ROMAN PERIOD
332 B.C. – A.D. 642

* Alexander the Great of Macedonia conquers Persian Empire and Egypt in 332 B.C.
* Alexander the Great founds the city of Alexandria in Egypt.
* After Alexander's death, his general Ptolemy becomes king.
* Egypt becomes a Roman province in 30 B.C.

HOW A MUMMY WAS MADE

THE ANCIENT EGYPTIANS BELIEVED THAT a person's life force could continue after death, but that it needed a body in which to dwell. To provide this, the dead person's own body was preserved, or mummified.

Special priests prepared the mummy. First, they used sharp knives to remove the body's internal organs. They put the liver, lungs, stomach, and intestines in containers called canopic jars, which would be buried with the mummy. The heart, believed to be the center of intelligence, was left in place. The brain was usually thrown away.

Next, the priests rinsed the body with spices, palm wine, and sweet-smelling oils. Then they covered it with natron, a type of salt that absorbs moisture, for about 40 days. Finally, the priests wrapped the dried-out body in layers of linen strips and then placed the mummy in a wooden coffin.

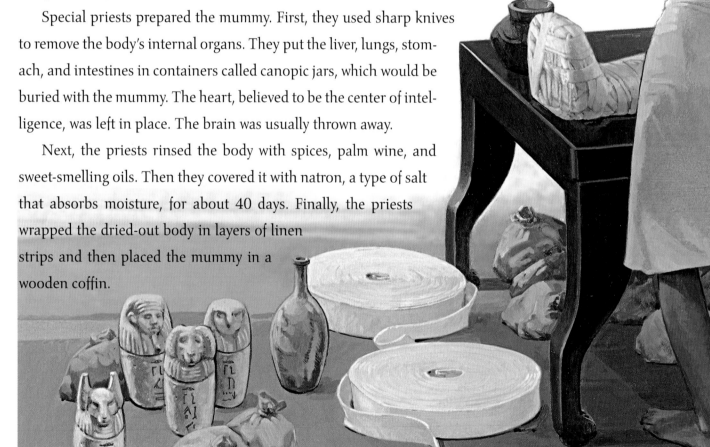

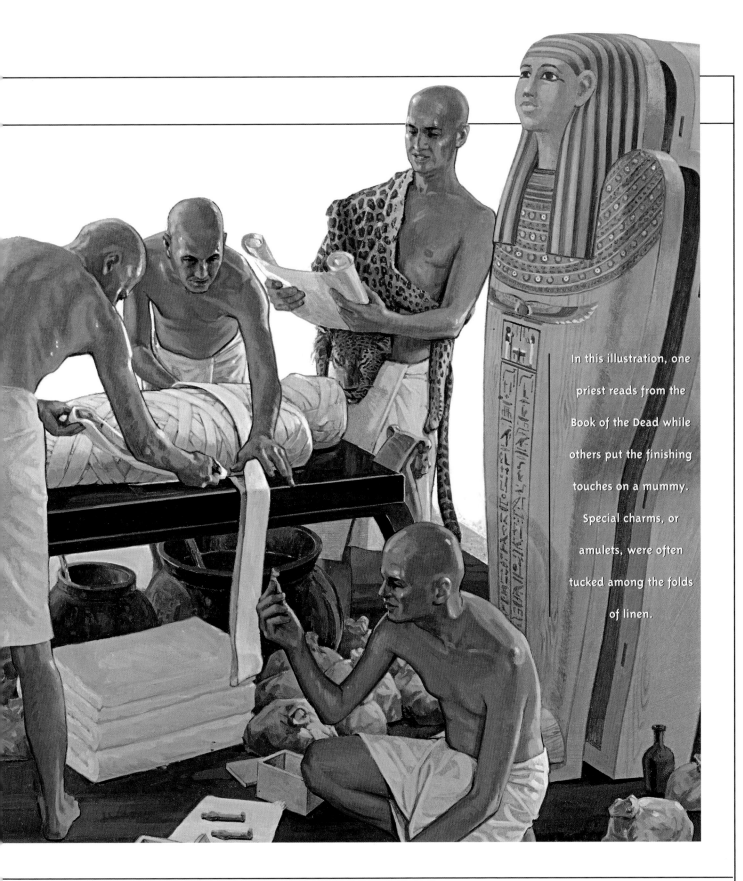

In this illustration, one priest reads from the Book of the Dead while others put the finishing touches on a mummy. Special charms, or amulets, were often tucked among the folds of linen.

GODS AND GODDESSES
OF ANCIENT EGYPT

ANCIENT EGYPTIANS WORSHIPED many different gods and goddesses. Some were local gods, sacred to a single town or village. Others were honored throughout the land. Here are some of the major gods and goddesses of ancient Egypt.

AMUN Often portrayed as a man wearing a crown with two feathered plumes, Amun was one of the most powerful gods. Over time, Amun merged with the sun god, Re, to become Amun-Re, king of the gods.

ANUBIS The god of the dead and mummification, Anubis had the head of a jackal (a type of wild dog that roamed cemeteries).

BASTET Ancient Egyptians appealed to this cat-headed goddess when they needed protection or help.

GEB Geb was the god of Earth. He is usually pictured together with Nut, the sky goddess who was both his sister and wife, and Shu, the god of air.

HATHOR This goddess was involved with many things, including love, women, music, and dancing. Hathor is often pictured as a cow or as a woman wearing a headdress of cow's horns cupping the sun. She was sometimes honored as the mother of the pharaoh.

HORUS A sky god with the head of a falcon, Horus was the son of the goddess Isis and the god Osiris. Horus was closely linked with each ruling pharaoh.

ISIS Wife of Osiris and mother of Horus, the goddess Isis symbolized the loyal wife and mother. Worshiped as a protective goddess, Isis is often shown wearing a throne-shaped headdress (which is also the hieroglyph for her name).

MAAT Truth, justice, and universal order were associated with the goddess Maat. She was also thought to control the seasons and the movements of the stars.

MIN Min was the god of fertility.

NUT The arching body of Nut, the sky goddess, made up the heavens. Nut was married to her brother Geb, god of Earth. According to legend, Nut swallowed the sun-god Re at the end of every day and gave birth to him every morning.

OSIRIS God of the dead, Osiris ruled in the world of the afterlife. He was the husband of Isis and the father of Horus. His brother was Seth.

PTAH Ptah was a creator god. He was worshiped by craftsmen.

RE Also known as Ra, Re was the all-powerful sun god. He is portrayed as a falcon-headed man crowned by a sun disk. Over time, Re merged with Amun to become Amun-Re, king of the gods.

SETH Seth was the god of violence and storms. According to legend, he killed his brother Osiris. He is often pictured with an animal-like head.

SHU Shu was the god of air. He is shown standing between the sky goddess, Nut, and the Earth god, Geb, to keep them apart.

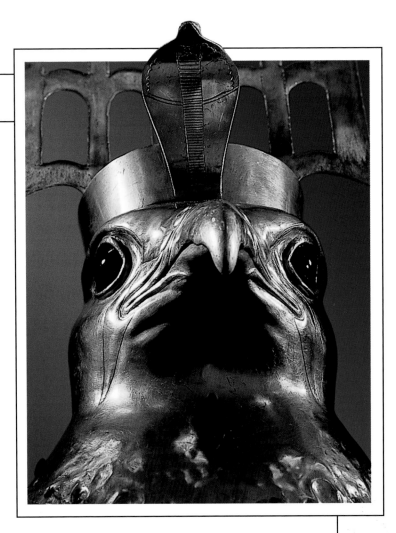

Made more than 5,000 years ago, this golden statue of the falcon god Horus suggests great power. The god's eyes were said to be the sun and the moon.

SOBEK The crocodile-headed god Sobek was linked with water and fertility.

THOTH The god Thoth was connected with writing, wisdom, and magic. He had the head of an ibis (a heron-like bird) and was pictured with a writing tablet. The baboon was sacred to him.

GLOSSARY

THIS GLOSSARY FEATURES WORDS FOUND IN THIS BOOK, as well as a variety of other terms that make it a fun place to browse if you're looking for more information on ancient Egypt.

AFTERLIFE an existence after death

ALEXANDRIA the capital of ancient Egypt during Greek and Roman times

AMULET a charm worn as protection against bad luck or evil spirits

ANCESTORS members of one's family who lived a long time ago

ANTECHAMBER a room used as an entrance to another room

ANTIQUITIES objects from ancient times

ARCHAEOLOGIST a person who practices archaeology

ARCHAEOLOGY the science of studying people who lived in the past by digging up old buildings and objects and examining them carefully

ARTIFACT an object that is made by humans

BAHARIYA OASIS an oasis southwest of Cairo. Site of the Valley of the Golden Mummies, a cemetery built when the Greeks and Romans ruled Egypt.

BOOK OF THE DEAD a collection of magic spells to protect the dead in the afterlife. The spells were usually written on papyrus and placed in the coffin alongside the dead body.

BURIAL CHAMBER the room in a tomb where the body is kept

CAIRO the present-day capital city of Egypt

CANOPIC JARS four special jars that held a mummy's internal organs (liver, lungs, stomach, and intestines)

CEMETERY a place where dead people are buried

CHAMBER another name for a room

CIVILIZATION a highly developed stage of human organization and culture

COFFIN a container in which a dead person is placed for burial; also called a casket

CULTURE the way of life, ideas, customs, and traditions of a group of people

CURSE an evil spell intended to cause harm

DELTA the fan-shaped area of rich soil deposited by a river where it flows into a larger body of water. The part of Egypt centered on the Nile Delta is known as Lower Egypt.

DYNASTY a series of rulers probably belonging to the same family. Thirty-one dynasties of kings and queens ruled Egypt between 3000 B.C. and 332 B.C.

EGYPTOLOGIST a scientist who studies ancient Egypt

EMBALM to preserve a dead body to protect it from decay

EXCAVATE to dig in the earth in search of ancient remains

FAMINE a severe lack of food

GILDED covered with gold

GIZA ancient Egyptian site on a rocky plateau near present-day city of Cairo. Site of the Great Pyramid and the Great Sphinx.

GRANITE a very hard stone

HEMATITE a mineral used by ancient Egyptians to make paint

HIEROGLYPHS the oldest form of Egyptian writing, consisting of symbols and pictures that represent sounds, words, and ideas

IMMORTALITY everlasting life

INSCRIPTION a message in letters or picture writing, often carved onto stone tombs or monuments

LABYRINTH a network of complicated passageways; also called a maze

LIMESTONE a rock that is used in building and carving. It is usually white or honey-colored.

LOWER EGYPT the part of Egypt centered on the Nile Delta

MAZE a network of complicated passageways; also called a labyrinth

MEMPHIS ancient capital city of Egypt

MIDDLE KINGDOM time period in Egyptian history covering the years 2040–1640 B.C.

MONUMENT a building or statue that is designed to remind people of a person or event

MORTUARY TEMPLE a building where priests held rituals to honor the spirit of the dead

MUD BRICK a brick made of mud, used to build many types of structures

MUMMIFY to preserve a dead body by drying it so it will last for a very long time. Egyptian mummies are usually dried with a salt called natron and wrapped in linen.

MUMMY a dried and preserved dead body

NATRON a type of salt used to dry out a dead body in order to mummify it

NECROPOLIS a large cemetery in an ancient city

NEW KINGDOM time period in Egyptian history covering the years 1550–1070 B.C. King Tutankhamun lived in this period.

NILE the world's longest river, which runs through Egypt on its path to the Mediterranean Sea

OASIS a place in the desert where there is water. Plants usually grow there.

OLD KINGDOM time period in Egyptian history covering the years 2650–2150 B.C. The greatest pyramids were built then.

ORGAN a part of the body that does a specific job, such as the heart, lungs, brain, stomach, and liver

PAPYRUS a kind of thick paper made from the stems of a water plant known by the same name. Ancient Egyptians wrote on papyrus.

PHARAOH starting in the New Kingdom, a term used for "king" in ancient Egypt

PLASTER a material made of lime, sand, and water that is often used by builders to coat inside walls. Tomb builders in ancient Egypt used plaster to seal doorways.

PRIEST in ancient Egypt, an official who performed religious ceremonies, including the preparation and burial of the dead

PYRAMID a structure with a square base and four sloping triangular sides that meet at a point on top. Kings of the Old and Middle Kingdoms were buried in pyramids.

RITUAL a set of special actions that are part of a religious ceremony

SACRED holy

SACRILEGE an action that shows disrespect for something sacred

SAQQARA the main necropolis for the ancient capital of Memphis

SARCOPHAGUS a large stone coffin that often holds smaller coffins

SCARAB an amulet or stamp carved to look like the dung beetle of the same name. Ancient Egyptians honored the scarab as a symbol of rebirth.

SCRIBE an official writer whose job included copying ancient scrolls; recording dates, events, and the names of rulers; sending messages; and counting cattle

SERDAB a small enclosed chamber within a tomb that usually contains a statue of the person buried in the tomb

SHRINE a sacred place or a container that holds holy objects

SPHINX a figure with a human head and a lion's body. The sphinx symbolized royal power in ancient Egypt. The most famous example is the Great Sphinx at Giza.

TEMPLE a building used for worship

THEBES the ancient name for the Egyptian city now known as Luxor. It is across the Nile from the Valley of the Kings, where King Tutankhamun's tomb was discovered.

TOMB the place where a dead body is buried. Tombs are often dug into rock or dirt.

USHABTI a small figure of a servant or farm worker placed in a tomb. Its purpose was to perform chores for its dead owner in the afterlife. Also called a shawabti.

VALLEY OF THE GOLDEN MUMMIES the site of a cemetery in the Bahariya Oasis, built when the Greeks and Romans ruled Egypt

VALLEY OF THE KINGS a valley west of Thebes that was used as a burial place for pharaohs of the New Kingdom

VIZIER the highest-ranking official after the pharaoh

BIBLIOGRAPHY

THE FOLLOWING BOOKS and articles were consulted for Part II and for many of the picture captions in this book:

Ancient Egypt: Discovering Its Splendors. National Geographic Society. Washington, D.C.: National Geographic Society, 1978.

Berger, Melvin, and Gilda Berger. *Mummies of the Pharaohs: Exploring the Valley of the Kings.* Washington, D.C.: National Geographic Society, 2001.

Conover, Adele. "Unraveling the Secrets of Egyptian Mummies." *National Geographic for Kids.* Winter 2001, 16–17.

Dumatt, Albert. "Mummies: The Inside Story." *National Geographic World,* June 1999, 6–9.

Fagan, Brian. *Egypt of the Pharaohs.* Washington, D.C.: National Geographic Society, 2001.

Gore, Rick. "Pharaohs of the Sun." *National Geographic,* April 2001, 34–57.

Hawass, Zahi. "Egypt's Hidden Tombs Revealed." *National Geographic,* September 2001, 32–41.

Hawass, Zahi, as told to Margaret Zackowitz. "The Mummy Hunter." *National Geographic World,* March 2002, 22–25.

Hawass, Zahi. *Valley of the Golden Mummies.* New York: Harry N. Abrams, 2000.

Miller, Peter. "Riddle of the Pyramid Boats." *National Geographic,* April 1988, 534–550.

Morell, Virginia. "The Pyramid Builders." *National Geographic,* November 2001, 78–99.

Pemberton, Delia. *Egyptian Mummies: People from the Past.* San Diego, Calif.: Harcourt, Inc., 2000.

Price, Sean. "Treasures of the Tomb: Discovering King Tut's Incredible Riches." *NG Kids,* November 2002, 20–23.

Reeves, Nicholas. *The Complete Tutankhamun.* London: Thomas and Hudson, 1990.

Treasures of Egypt. National Geographic Collector's Edition Vol. 5. Washington, D.C.: National Geographic Society, 2003.

Webster, Donovan. "Valley of the Mummies." *National Geographic,* October 1999, 76–87.

Weeks, Kent. R. "Valley of the Kings." *National Geographic,* September 1998, 2–33.

Williams, A. R. "Death on the Nile." *National Geographic,* October 2002, 2–25.

FURTHER READING

HERE ARE MORE BOOKS that provide lots of fascinating information about archaeology and ancient Egypt:

Ancient Civilizations, 2500 BC—AD 500 (Time-Life Student Library series). By the editors of Time-Life Books. Alexandria, Va.: Time-Life Books, 1998.

Ardagh, Philip. *Ancient Egypt* (History Detectives series). New York: Peter Bedrick Books, 2000.

Hawass, Zahi. *Hidden Treasures of Ancient Egypt: Unearthing the Masterpieces of the Egyptian Museum in Cairo.* Washington, D.C.: National Geographic Society, 2004.

Hawass, Zahi. *Secrets from the Sand: My Search for Egypt's Past.* New York: Harry N. Abrams, 2003.

Honan, Linda. *Spend the Day in Ancient Egypt: Projects and Activities That Bring the Past to Life.* New York: John Wiley & Sons, Inc., 1999.

Ikram, Salima, and Aidan Dodson. *The Mummy in Ancient Egypt: Equipping the Dead for Eternity.* New York: Thames and Husdon, 1998.

Kamrin, Janice. *Ancient Egyptian Hieroglyphs: A Practical Guide.* New York: Abrams Books, 2004.

Macauley, David. *Pyramid.* New York: Houghton Mifflin Company, 1982.

MacDonald, Fiona. *Mummies and Tombs.* New York: Lorenz Books, 2000.

Morris, Neil. *Ancient Egypt.* New York: Peter Bedrick Books, 2000.

Shaw, Ian. *The Oxford History of Ancient Egypt.* New York: Oxford University Press Inc., 2002.

WEB SITES

CHECK OUT THESE WEB SITES for fun facts and up-to-date information:

Ancient Egypt
www.ancientegypt.co.uk/menu.html
The British Museum's guide to ancient Egyptian history

Egypt History
www.arab.net/egypt/history/egypt_history.html
Egypt's complete history, from predynastic times to the present

Egyptian Mummies
www.si.edu/resource/faq/nmnh/mummies.htm
An overview of the ancient mummification process

Life in Ancient Egypt
www.carnegiemuseums.org/cmnh/exhibits/egypt/index.html
Describes what life was like in ancient Egypt

At the Tomb of Tutankhamun
www.nationalgeographic.com/egypt/
Interactive edition of a 1923 *National Geographic* article about Tut's tomb

The Plateau
www.guardians.net/hawass/index.htm
The official Web site of Dr. Zahi Hawass

The Pronunciation of Ancient Egyptian
www.friesian.com/egypt.htm
All about the ancient Egyptian language

Pyramids: The Inside Story
www.pbs.org/wgbh/nova/pyramid
An interactive tour of the pyramids

Tour Egypt
www.touregypt.net
A guide to ancient and modern Egypt

I N D E X

This gold-covered carving of a lioness's head topped a bedpost found in King Tut's tomb.

One of the world's largest nonprofit scientific and educational organizations, the National Geographic Society was founded in 1888 "for the increase and diffusion of geographic knowledge." Fulfilling this mission, the Society educates and inspires millions every day through its magazines, books, television programs, videos, maps and atlases, research grants, the National Geographic Bee, teacher workshops, and innovative classroom materials. The Society is supported through membership dues, charitable gifts, and income from the sale of its educational products. This support is vital to National Geographic's mission to increase global understanding and promote conservation of our planet through exploration, research, and education.

For more information, please call 1-800-NGS LINE (647-5463) or write to the following address:
National Geographic Society
1145 17th Street N.W.
Washington, D.C. 20036-4688 U.S.A.
Visit the Society's Web site at www.nationalgeographic.com.

INDEX